Response to Intervention

The Guilford Practical Intervention in the Schools Series

Kenneth W. Merrell, Series Editor

Books in this series address the complex academic, behavioral, and social–emotional needs of children and youth at risk. School-based practitioners are provided with practical, research-based, and readily applicable tools to support students and team successfully with teachers, families, and administrators. Each volume is designed to be used directly and frequently in planning and delivering clinical services. Features include a convenient format to facilitate photocopying, step-by-step instructions for assessment and intervention, and helpful, timesaving reproducibles.

Response to Intervention

Principles and Strategies
for Effective Practice

RACHEL BROWN-CHIDSEY
MARK W. STEEGE

THE GUILFORD PRESS
New York   London

© 2005 The Guilford Press
A Division of Guilford Publications, Inc.
72 Spring Street, New York, NY 10012
www.guilford.com

Printed in Canada

This book is printed on acid-free paper.

Last digit is print number: 9 8 7 6 5 4

Library of Congress Cataloging-in-Publication Data

Brown-Chidsey, Rachel.
  Response to intervention : principles and strategies for effective practice / Rachel Brown-
Chidsey, Mark W. Steege.
    p. cm.
  Includes bibliographical references and index.
  ISBN-10 1-59385-215-0   ISBN-13 978-1-59385-215-3 (pbk.)
  1. Remedial teaching. 2. Slow learning children—Education. I. Steege, Mark W.   II. Title.
  LB1029.R4B76 2005
  371.9—dc22

                                                                              2005017004

About the Authors

Rachel Brown-Chidsey, PhD, is Associate Professor of School Psychology at the University of Southern Maine. Prior to obtaining her doctorate at the University of Massachusetts–Amherst, she taught middle and high school history and special education for 10 years. Her research areas include curriculum-based measurement, response to intervention, and scientifically based reading instruction methods. Dr. Brown-Chidsey participated in the 2002 Multi-Site Conference on the Future of School Psychology and subsequently edited *Assessment for Intervention: A Problem-Solving Approach* (Guilford Press, 2005), which stemmed from the research presented at the conference. Dr. Brown-Chidsey is a nationally certified school psychologist and a licensed psychologist, and she has served on the Maine Advisory Board for School Psychological Service Providers and the Maine Task Force for Special Education Eligibility.

Mark W. Steege, PhD, is Professor and Clinical Coordinator in the School Psychology Program at the University of Southern Maine. Dr. Steege earned his doctorate at the University of Iowa and completed postdoctoral work as a pediatric psychologist at the University of Iowa College of Medicine. His research areas include functional behavioral assessment, interventions for individuals with developmental disabilities, and assessment of autism spectrum disorders. Dr. Steege coauthored *Conducting School-Based Functional Behavioral Assessments: A Practitioner's Guide* (Guilford Press, 2003), with T. Steuart Watson, and has published numerous articles related to applied behavior analysis, functional behavioral assessment, and single-subject research design.

Preface

This book is designed to prepare teachers, psychologists, and other educational specialists to understand and use response to intervention (RTI) methods in schools. Recent federal legislation mandating the application of an RTI model has raised the profile of these methods considerably, but RTI principles and strategies have been around for a long time and are based on basic scientific methods. In essence, we propose that scientific methods can be used in schools on a daily basis to select, use, and review the instructional practices in classrooms. When student learning outcomes indicate that students are making effective progress, no changes are suggested. When student data show that one or more students are not making progress, then changes to the instruction need to be made to find the right intervention that yields effective outcomes for all students.

Our approach to RTI involves 10 primary steps, but not all students will need all the steps; indeed, most students will participate in no more than three steps. But for those students who are at risk for school difficulties, the remaining seven steps offer a scientific method for identifying what type(s) of instruction work for them and how intensive such instruction needs to be. In the United States, special education was implemented in 1975 to ensure that *all* students, regardless of ability, have access to a free public education. Since then, many students have benefited from special education, but others have not. In some cases, the interventions used in special education have been no more effective than those in general education. In other settings, the number of students receiving special education far exceeds the actual prevalence of the disabilities identified.

Several recent federal initiatives have focused on reducing the number of students receiving special education. While this is not an appropriate end unto itself, RTI methods can assist educators in determining what instructional practices work with which students so that all children have access to the education they need. RTI has been described elsewhere as "essential education science" (Brown-Chidsey, 2005c). We propose that if RTI methods are used systematically and consistently, more students will find success in general and special education in all schools and districts. Some students will need specialized instruction, and when data indicate that only specialized instruction yields success for a given student, special education is the best answer. Many more students do not need special education but do need to learn how to read, write, and compute; RTI can show educators about the progress their students are making and whether instructional changes are needed.

We wrote this book to give school psychologists and educators the tools necessary to understand RTI methods for academic problems and to develop and implement effective interventions in their schools. We have provided numerous assessment forms, overhead slides, and other reproducible materials to assist in both training and daily practice; supplemental materials for the book can also be found online at www.guilford.com/rti.

Contents

List of Figures, Tables, Boxes, Forms, and Overheads

FIGURES

TABLES

BOXES

FORMS

OVERHEADS

1

Introduction

What Is Response to Intervention (RTI)?

Consider the case of Sean. Sean is a first grader who has not yet developed important prereading skills that he will need if he wants to succeed in school, graduate, go to college, or get a well-paying job in the future. His parents, his teacher, his principal, and the superintendent of his school district want him to learn how to read. So Sean keeps plugging away in school, sitting attentively when his teacher reads to the class, pointing to pictures in books when his parents read to him at home, and "borrowing" answers from other student's worksheets when completing class assignments. At the end of Sean's first-grade year he takes a test to show what he has learned during the year. The test shows that he knows his colors and shapes, but he still cannot read.

Sean's teacher makes a note about his reading problems in his file before it is sent on to the second-grade teacher. When Sean starts the second grade his teacher is already concerned about his reading difficulties, and she works with him closely for several weeks. At the end of October, his teacher has concluded that Sean must have a learning disability, so she refers him for evaluation. In early January an individualized education plan (IEP) meeting about Sean is held. At the meeting, results from the evaluation are reported. These results show that Sean scored in the low end of the average range on both academic achievement and cognitive (IQ) testing. As a result of these highly consistent scores, Sean's parents are told that their son does not have a learning disability. The parents are relieved to hear that, but then ask, "Who will help our son learn to read?" The assistant principal who is chairing the meeting regretfully tells Sean's parents that, because his school does not have Title I funding and Sean did not qualify for special education, he will have to keep "trying" to learn to read in his current class. Sean's mom starts to cry, and his dad stands up and states angrily, "This is crazy! Our son cannot read, but you won't do anything to help him! We're leaving and I'm calling the superintendent."

The foregoing scenario is neither uncommon nor unlikely. In our experience as educators and psychologists we have evaluated and met with the parents of many students who had clear and specific learning needs but could not obtain additional school assistance to meet those needs. The described example is sometimes known as a "waiting-to-fail" model, because Sean may eventually qualify for special education if he continues to lag behind in reading and cannot engage with or participate in reading-based classroom activities. The tragedy of this model is that by the time Sean meets the criteria for special education eligibility, the best years for teaching him to read will have passed (Snow, Burns, & Griffin, 1998).

The good news for students like Sean is that the instructional methods and educational policies needed to get him the reading (or math, or writing) instruction that he needs are available. The instructional methods and assessment procedures most likely to benefit students like Sean are known as *response to intervention* (RTI). RTI is an assessment–intervention model that allows schools to deliver sound instructional methods to students like Sean who otherwise might fall through the cracks. This book is designed to provide knowledge, skills, and resources for using RTI methods in schools. RTI is a relatively new term for an approach to understanding and addressing students' school difficulties. For the purpose of clarity in this book, we developed the following definition. First, let's define the important words in the term:

Response: 1. The act of responding
                 2. An answer or reply
Intervention: 1. The act of intervening; interposition
                 2. Any interference that may affect the interests of others, especially of one or more states with the affairs of another; mediation

Essentially, RTI is an objective examination of the cause–effect relationship(s) between academic or behavioral *intervention* and the student's *response* to the intervention. For example, a student's *response* to a specific reading instruction *intervention* can be measured using oral reading fluency indicators. When the core terms *response* and *intervention* are put together, a more general set of educational practices and procedures can be defined. Such practices include providing a specific *intervention* (an interference that affects others) for one or more students and measuring the student(s)' *response* (answer or reply) to the intervention. Put more succinctly, RTI is a systematic and data-based method for identifying, defining, and resolving students' academic and/or behavior difficulties. This definition has certain inherent limitations. For example, it includes only academic and behavior problems. We chose to include only academic interventions in this book, because this is an important and emerging application of RTI procedures. Specifically, the most recent version of the Individuals with Disabilities Education Improvement Act (IDEIA, 2004) included RTI references related to identification of learning disabilities. This use of RTI has widespread implications for many aspects of education, and this book will focus on what both general and special education professionals need to know about RTI. Importantly, RTI is designed to take the guesswork out of the assessment and intervention process as it is implemented first in general education, and then, for a small number of students, in special education.

HISTORY

The components that make up RTI methods have been used in schools for many years but have not been understood as part of the larger system now known as RTI. For example, teachers have routinely used targeted methods of instruction to help individual students develop certain skills. Likewise, as standard practices, schools have reported on student progress at regular intervals. What makes RTI different from these prior means of helping students is that the assessment and instruction practices are integrated into an objective data-based system with built-in decision stages. This is in contrast to past models of student assessment in which students were assumed to be doing OK unless identified otherwise (Fletcher, Coulter, Reschly, & Vaughn, 2004). In RTI, all students are screened and monitored for specific educational outcomes, and those needing additional assistance are given targeted intervention that is monitored systematically using scientifically based data recording procedures. In essence, RTI integrates high-quality teaching and assessment methods in a systematic way so that students who are not successful when presented with one set of instructional methods can be given the chance to succeed with the use of other practices.

KEY FEATURES OF RTI

As described in the RTI definition above, there are two main components that distinguish RTI from other teaching and assessment practices. These essential components are *systematic* and *data-based* activities. A conceptual framework of our RTI model is given in Figure 1.1. The figure includes an inverted triangle with three sections, which reflect three tiers of intervention in RTI. Tier 1 is at the top of the figure and reflects the general education curriculum. This tier is designed for and provided to all students in each grade level. Tier 1 is comprehensive and universal. As will be discussed in detail in later chapters, Tier 1 activities are selected on the basis of effectiveness. Still, not all students will respond to Tier 1 instruction with success. Tier 2 is the middle section of the figure and represents those students who need more intensive and specific instruction in order to be successful in school. Importantly, in our figure, data are the only connecting point, or pathway, between each tier. A student can cross between tiers only when data indicate that it needs to happen. A third tier is found at the bottom of the figure, which represents a small subset of students who do not respond to the interventions provided in Tiers 1 and 2. Tier 3 activities include comprehensive assessment to identify whether a student has a specific disability and meets the criteria for special education. Notably, Tier 3 does not include special education services; rather, it is a transition point for those students who have not yet found success in school.

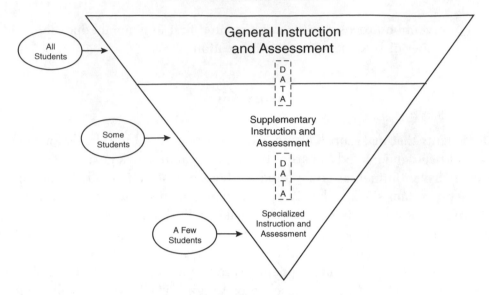

FIGURE 1.1. RTI model.

Our model of RTI is built upon previous work related to school assessment and instruction. An early precursor to RTI methods is Deno's "cascade" model of special education service delivery (Deno, 1970). In this model Deno conceptualized students' educational progress as "developmental capital" that could yield dividends in response to appropriate instruction in the least restrictive environment. Deno's "cascade" features increasingly small instructional groupings matched to the individual student's specific needs. Deno's model (1970) was used as a core framework for the implementation of special education regulations during the 1970s and 1980s (Brown-Chidsey, Seppala, & Segura, 2000). While this model helped to make special education a reality for many students, one of the problems seen in special education, starting in the 1980s, was the rapid increase in students identified as having learning disabilities (McBride, Dumont, & Willis, 2004).

In part to address the rapid increase in special education placements, several programs and initiatives have been implemented to address the needs of students before they are given special education services. The first of these attempts was known as the regular education initiative, or REI (Hallahan, Keller, McKinney, Lloyd, & Bryan, 1988; Jenkins, Pious, & Jewell, 1990). This federal policy focused on having as many students as possible remain in "regular" education (Ackerman, 1987). Drawing from Deno's cascade model, the idea was to focus on determination of what constituted the least restrictive environment for students with disabilities. Instead of assuming that all students with disabilities would need separate specialized teaching, the REI effort pushed teachers and administrators to keep as many children in their original classrooms as possible (McLeskey & Skiba, 1990).

The REI was criticized from its first days, with concerns ranging from lack of teacher training (Coates, 1989; Semmel & Abernathy, 1991) to violation of student rights (Bryan,

Bay, & Donahue, 1988; Chisholm, 1988). Jenkins et al. (1990) noted that the REI was an attempt to make sense of the regular and special education continuum (Drame, 2002). Analysis showed that the REI was not very effective in reducing the number of students receiving special education services (D'Alonzo & Boggs, 1990; National Center for Education Statistics, 2004; Peltier, 1993). Soon after REI measures were put into place, a second major push to reform special education was begun. Known as "inclusive education," this movement had longer-lasting effects than REI (Fuchs & Fuchs, 1994; Kubicek, 1994). This effort to change special education policies and practices was focused more on establishing the rights and needs of students with disabilities than reducing the overall number of students receiving special education services (Kavale, 2002). The inclusion movement led to examinations of how special education services were being provided (Evans, 1990). As with RTI, many researchers suggested that additional training was needed by general education classroom teachers (Murphy, 1996; Taylor & Richards, 1997). Most notably, educators were reported to be philosophically supportive of special education but not adequately trained to meet the needs of students with disabilities in inclusive classrooms (Villa & Thousand, 1996).

Although the inclusion movement has not totally disappeared, recent efforts to address the large number of students in special education have shifted to using RTI methods as the primary mechanism. Additionally, the reduction efforts are now squarely focused on reducing the number of students identified with learning disabilities rather than reducing special education enrollments overall. Kavale and Forness (2000) have suggested that the reason why both REI and inclusion failed to bring about the desired changes in general and special education is that they failed to utilize empirical evidence of effective practices and instead focused on philosophical issues about the moral imperative to educate all children. Of note, Kavale (2003) expressed opposition to adoption of RTI policies at the federal level until more evidence was produced that such practices systematically result in desired outcomes. Kavale's criticism of current RTI methods appears to be an extension of the arguments made against REI and inclusion. Kavale and others have argued that until there is clear and substantial evidence that RTI methods produce large-scale improvements in educational outcomes, RTI should not be used at the state or national level.

The problem with waiting to implement RTI on a large scale is that the only way to determine whether it will achieve its promise is to implement it at the state or national level. Such implementation needs to be done with the rights and needs of students uppermost in mind. Importantly, RTI methods include certain "safety net" features that can prevent negative consequences. For example, unlike REI and inclusion, RTI is by definition data-driven, so no decisions are made without evidence to support them. Most importantly, RTI is not simply one intervention or method. It is a set of scientifically based procedures that can be used to make decisions about educational programs. In light of the history of efforts to improve educational outcomes for all students, it is important that current and future such initiatives not get bogged down in rhetoric. As noted by Hart and Risley (1995), early intervention has a huge effect on long-term outcomes. For this reason, this book focuses on specific RTI procedures for individual students. It is designed to be a handbook and implementation manual for those who seek to use RTI on a regular, ongoing basis.

RTI AND PROBLEM SOLVING

By their nature, RTI methods are problem-solving activities. Although many students and teachers in schools may not perceive their daily experiences as "problems," they do engage in ongoing assessment and reflection. In the course of daily events, teachers (and students) are generally pleased when teaching and learning activities go as expected. Under such circumstances, no major "problems" are evident. When a teacher notices that a student's work is not what was expected, a different reaction is likely to occur. If the teacher find the student's work to be exemplary, he or she may offer additional praise. If the teacher finds the work to be below expectations, he or she may believe that a learning problem is present. Such a problem could include academic skills such as reading, writing, or math, or it could relate to behavioral expectations such as whether the student is able to stay seated, stand in line, or play with others at recess. Regardless of the event, teachers and students tend not to notice school problems until they occur, and then they are very apparent. As a result of efforts to help all students be successful in school, researchers have developed specific problem-solving methods designed to assist teachers and specialists when school difficulties arise (Brown-Chidsey, 2005a; Deno, 2002; Tilly, 2002).

RTI methods are closely linked with problem-solving models for school difficulties. In this volume, Deno's five-part data-based problem-solving model will be used as part of the RTI stages and activities (Deno, 2005). A summary of the problem-solving model is found in Table 1.1. This model includes (1) problem identification, (2) problem definition, (3) designing intervention plans, (4) implementing the intervention, and (5) problem solution. As shown in Table 1.1, each of these steps is aligned with specific assessment and instructional activities designed to reduce or eliminate a student's school difficulties. This model is designed to be used continuously and interactively. As one step ends, the next

TABLE 1.1. A Data-Based Problem-Solving Model

Problem-solving steps	Assessment procedures	Evaluation decisions
1. Problem identification	Observing/recording student performance	Does a problem exist?
2. Problem definition	Quantifying the perceived discrepancy	Is the problem important?
3. Designing intervention plans	Exploring alternative goals and solution hypotheses	What is the best solution hypothesis?
4. Implementing the intervention	Monitoring fidelity of intervention and data collection	Is the solution attempt progressing as planned?
5. Problem solution	Requantifying the discrepancy	Is the original problem being solved though this attempted solution?

Note. From Deno (2005, p. 25). Copyright 2005 by The Guilford Press. Reprinted by permission.

begins. In some cases, not all steps will be implemented. In other cases, each step will be utilized multiple times to help identify the best way to help a student be successful in school. An important feature of this problem-solving model is that it recognizes that schools cannot be problem-free. Instead, it offers a way of dealing with problems when they happen so that the long-term negative impact is minimized.

Problem Identification

The first step begins with problem identification activities. Such activities include any and all moments when a student's school difficulties are initially identified. To help explain this step and the other steps of the model, the metaphor of radar will be used. Problem identification may be likened to the moment when something is first detected on a radar screen. Those monitoring the screen do not know what's causing the "blip" on the screen, but they know it needs to be addressed. A number of different people may participate in problem identification activities. Teachers, parents, students, administrators, bus drivers, and/or cafeteria staff members may help to bring problems to greater attention and put them on the "radar screen." Problem identification is not an end unto itself. Instead, this first step activates a process by which more data about a student's school difficulties can be collected.

Problem Definition

The second step of the problem-solving model is problem definition. This step includes evaluating the nature and magnitude of the problem and determining whether the problem requires an intervention or might resolve itself on its own. This is similar to what seafarers and aviators must do in order to determine whether the radar signal is from a large attack ship or a small unarmed private vessel. How the pilot responds will be based on the nature of the object identified by the radar. In the same way, educators can help students by defining the nature of the student's problem. Problem definition activities include evaluating the student's skills in certain areas and comparing them to what is expected. Such definitions include measurements such as reading fluency, frequency of on-task behaviors, and rate of homework completion. Only once a student's current behaviors have been identified is it possible to know the magnitude and importance of the problem identified in Step 1. Some problems may be very small and likely to resolve on their own over time. Alternatively, other problems may be of immediate concern. If the difference between a student's current performance and what is expected is large, that student is likely to have a serious school problem that needs to be resolved.

Designing Intervention Plans

The third step of the problem-solving model includes putting in place specific activities and procedures designed to reduce significantly the difference between what a student can currently do and what he or she is expected to do. The development of such intervention plans is similar to how a pilot of a boat or plane might respond to information concerning the source of a radar signal. If the captain of a small sailboat is charting a course and finds that he or she is steering toward a much larger vessel, changing course is the prudent thing to do, especially if the larger ship is an aircraft carrier or oil tanker. Educators can help students to chart a new course by designing ways to improve their skills so that they can be successful in school. As will be discussed in Chapter 4, all interventions need to be empirically validated with evidence of effectiveness in school settings. Effective interventions include methods such as direct instruction of specific skills, positive behavior support plans (PBSPs), and peer-assisted learning strategies (PALSs). A specific time frame and plan for implementing the intervention, what personnel will be involved, and how data will be collected provide crucial links to the next steps of the problem-solving process.

Implementing the Intervention

This step of the model has two major components: implementation and progress monitoring. The intervention should be implemented as planned and intended. If a well-designed intervention is put into action incorrectly, it may be impossible to know whether it could have worked. For this reason, the intervention plan should include some form of treatment integrity check to document whether the plan was implemented as intended. If an intervention is implemented as planned but does not work, it can be changed, but information about initial ineffectiveness is needed in order to design effective alternatives. If some portions of the intervention did work, these might be retained and used with additional new components. The only way to know if an intervention works is to collect data. This is the critical second component of problem-solving step 4. From the very first moment that an intervention is put into place, data concerning the outcomes must be collected. This is no different from a pilot who would monitor the radar screen as well as other sources of information to verify that the threat posed by a larger vessel is reduced as a result of someone changing course. Data collection methods can include recording the frequency, rate, accuracy, duration, and intensity of a behavior or skill (Watson & Steege, 2003). Determination of what type of data recording procedure to use is based on the specific nature of the problem. Students who are often off-task can be monitored according to the frequency of on-task behaviors. Students with reading difficulties can be monitored by checking and recording oral or silent reading fluency (Brown-Chidsey, Davis, & Maya, 2003). Progress monitoring also involves ongoing data analysis. Single-case experimental designs (e.g., Steege, Brown-Chidsey, & Mace, 2002) are typically used in the analysis of data.

Problem Solution

As mentioned earlier, the problem-solving model is organized in such a way that it can be used to solve a wide range of school problems. It is set up to account for the reality that there will always be problems in schools. Thankfully, many school problems are solvable, and this model has an identifiable end step that documents when a problem is resolved.

The specific way that each school problem will be solved will always differ according to the strengths and needs of each child. The important aspect of the fifth, and final, step of the model is that it allows for recognition of school success by noting when certain preset criteria for success are met. Just as the captain of a boat lets out a sign of relief when a new course results in being out of harm's way, students and their support teams can determine a performance level that will mark problem solution and celebrate when it is met. As noted above, the problem-solving model is set up to be used continuously, as needed. For some students, one intervention may be all it takes to achieve problem solution. For others, the problems may be greater in size and number, and multiple problem solution parties will be shared on the pathway to greater success. Importantly, problem solution provides all members of the school team with the chance to identify what has been successful and develop new goals and plans.

RTI AND SPECIAL EDUCATION

As described at the beginning of this chapter, RTI methods share a legacy with prior efforts to improve special education programs. It is impossible to separate RTI completely from special education because RTI activities occur in a sequence along a continuum. When empirically validated interventions are used, it is expected that most students' school progress will be appropriate. Still, RTI methods include steps to be taken for students who continue to struggle in school despite attempted interventions. For some students, RTI activities will result in evaluation and eligibility for special education services. Indeed, as described in detail in Chapter 2, RTI methods have been included in the most recent reauthorization of the Individuals with Disabilities Education Act. Such methods also fit with other recent education policies such No Child Left Behind Act (NCLB, 2001) and related state programs. Importantly, RTI methods were developed with the goal of spreading a wide net for identification of students having difficulty in school. This net is designed initially to identify a larger number of students who need help than will end up in special education (O'Connor, 2003). The goal is to provide students at risk of or already experiencing school difficulties with interventions that prevent additional problems (Compton, 2003; Speece, Case, & Malloy, 2003).

An example of the wide-net approach included in RTI is the Texas Primary Reading Instrument (TPRI). This instrument is part of a statewide effort to identify and define the needs of students at risk of reading problems (Center for Academic and Reading Skills, 1999). It is organized such that scores on the TPRI will yield a list of students who may have reading problems. This list is used to design and implement reading interventions that will be monitored over time. It is expected that most students will show reading improvement as a result of the intervention. Those students who do not show improvement are provided with additional intervention that is developed in response to the data collected during the earlier program. Students who consistently struggle to learn to read despite multiple empirically based reading interventions are evaluated to determine whether they are eligible for special education services. Similar programs also have been used in Iowa and Massachusetts. Data from early reading RTI programs in Iowa showed that fewer students were ultimately placed in special education programs after RTI methods were used than before (Tilly, 2003).

RTI AND GENERAL EDUCATION

The success of RTI as a means of reducing the number of students who receive special education services is important for those concerned about too many students being identified as disabled. The more important aspect of RTI data thus far is how many students have found greater school success as a result of data-based educational programming. Yes, fewer students have been labeled as disabled; however, these same students have developed critical basic skills that increase the likelihood they will be successful in school and life. For this reason, RTI is really a general education initiative. RTI activities begin and end in general education. They may serve as a pathway for "child find" activities for some students, but they provide systematic, data-based decision making for far more general education students. Some researchers have noted that general educators are not prepared for the demands that are implicit in RTI methods (Fletcher et al., 2002; Fletcher, 2003; L. Fuchs, 2003; Kovaleski, 2003; Vaughn & Fuchs, 2003). Nonetheless, there is emerging evidence that RTI methods are very effective as part of general education, and the U.S. Department of Education's *Reading First* grant program is organized according to several RTI principles (Good, Simmons, & Kame'enui, 2001; U.S. Department of Education, 2002a).

In order for RTI to become a routine part of general education, teachers, administrators, and specialists will need to learn how to implement and interpret RTI methods and data. Some teachers may not have received much, if any, training in data analysis. Others may worry that RTI is another "add-on" to what they are already doing and fear that there are not enough hours in the school day to incorporate RTI practices. Importantly, RTI does not require "adding on" to what is already being done in the classroom. Instead, it involves reviewing current classroom practices to identify those that yield evidence of effective instruction as well as those that do not. RTI methods call for teachers to *replace* those practices that do not yield student improvement with those that do. When using RTI, general education teachers will remain the most important part of students' school success.

RTI AND PUBLIC POLICY

RTI has already become part of several educational policies and is likely to be incorporated into future programs as well. The rationale for having RTI as a central focus of public education policy is that it is a population-based system for determining which students need more assistance. Population-based decision making comes from the field of public health (Doll & Haack, 2005). Examples of population-based policies already widely in place include mandatory immunization of all school children, review and recall of beef, pork, and poultry by the Department of Agriculture, and warnings about alcohol use on beer, wine, and liquor labels. All of these polices are designed to protect the public health and welfare through systematic procedures, recalls, and warnings. Although population-based decision making has been widely used in health, food, and safety policies for many years, it has been less utilized in school settings. RTI represents a major application of population-bascd policy in education because it calls for screening of the entire school population for identification of possible school difficulties (Coyne, Kame'enui, Simmons, 2001, 2004; Coyne, Kame'enui, Simmons, & Harn, 2004).

Just as there are many public welfare benefits from immunizations, meat recalls, and alcohols labels, RTI applications in schools are likely to yield important gains for all students. The universal nature of RTI methods mean that all students are reviewed regularly to determine if school problems are present (Biglan, Mrazek, Carnine, & Flay, 2003). This prevents students from "slipping through the cracks." Those students who need additional assistance are provided with interventions previously shown to be effective, just as physicians use treatments validated in research studies. The data-driven nature of RTI means that decisions about school practices are derived from students' actual performance in class. New interventions are provided only as needed when data show that existing practices are not working. In the end, RTI is designed to enhance *all* students' educational outcomes by providing continuous progress monitoring of all students and specialized assistance to those who need it.

BIG IDEAS ABOUT RTI

There are three main components to RTI: high-quality instruction, frequent assessment, and data-based decision making (see Table 1.2). Each of these components connects to a "big idea" about educational policy. High-quality instruction is based on the idea that all children deserve effective instruction that leads to achieving functional skills. Frequent assessment is based on the idea that continuous assessment leads to skill improvement. Instructional decision making relates to the idea that adjustments to instruction must be based on data. When the three components of RTI are put together with the problem-solving assessment model, decisions about a student's progress toward education goals are much easier to make.

The remaining chapters of this book will provide detailed information about each component of RTI and how to use each to foster positive academic and behavior out-

TABLE 1.2. "Big Ideas" about RTI Methods

RTI component	"Big idea"
High-quality instruction	All children deserve effective instruction that leads to achieving functional skills.
Frequent assessment	Continuous assessment leads to skill improvement.
Data-based decision making	Adjustments to instruction must be based on data.

comes for all students. Chapters 2 and 3 provide information about the policy framework around which RTI procedures can be used. Chapter 4 includes a review of scientifically based educational practices and evidence-based instruction. Chapter 5 describes single-subject research designs and how they can be used in RTI practices. Chapters 6 and 7 detail the individual steps in RTI methods and show how they are applied in cases involving academic as well as behavior difficulties. Chapter 8 covers the use of RTI with students from diverse backgrounds. Chapters 9 and 10 offer information about how to use RTI as part of special education and to record and manage educational data and reports. Chapters 11 and 12 include training materials as well as answers to questions about RTI. It is hoped that readers will come away from this book with the knowledge and skills to design, implement, and evaluate RTI methods in school settings.

2

NCLB, IDEIA, and RTI

Linkages across National Education Policies

HISTORICAL CONTEXT OF RTI

Chapter 1 included information about the social and historical context in which RTI research and programs have evolved. Importantly, RTI is part of a larger effort to improve access to educational opportunities for all students. One of the core elements of RTI that is a very recent advance in the field of education is scientifically based practice. Scientifically based practice refers to those instructional methods and pedagogical approaches that have been verified by numerous research studies. The scientific basis of education practice also has been referred to in a number of studies as *evidence-based* practice (Kratochwill & Stoiber, 2002). The meaning intended by referring to certain educational methods as evidence-based is to help all educators understand the importance of scientifically based data in validating instructional practices. Although educational research has been conducted for many, many years, the use of such data to inform and change instructional practices is much more limited (Pressley, Duke, & Boling, 2004; Sweet, 2004)

Thanks to research advances in the area of reading, there now exists a strong body of evidence about typical and atypical reading development (Lyon, Shaywitz, & Chhabra, 2004; McCardle & Chhabra, 2004; Shaywitz, 2003). The consistency and high quality of the research produced about reading led a number of policymakers and researchers to push for heavier emphasis on a scientific basis for any and all instructional methods used in schools. Two recent U.S. education policies have incorporated requirements for evidence-based practices as required elements. The two programs requiring evidence-based practices are the No Child Left Behind ACT (NCLB) of 2001 and the Individuals with Disabilities Education Improvement Act (IDEIA) reauthorization of 2004. Additionally, there is specific language about an evidence basis for instructional and assessment conducted as part of the Reading First grant program, which is a subpart of NCLB. When reviewed as a set, these legislated programs include language that sets up a policy framework in which RTI methods are expected to be an essential feature of educational practice throughout the United States. These legislative policies will be reviewed in turn.

RTI COMPONENTS IN NCLB

No Child Left Behind

No Child Left Behind is the name of the reauthorization of the Elementary and Secondary Education Act (ESEA), first passed in 1965. ESEA was the first major U.S. federal legislation to provide funding to public schools. The thrust behind the 1965 act was a group of policies collectively known as the "Great Society" (Halperin, 1979; Sweet, 2004). Begun under the Kennedy administration and completed by the Johnson administration, these programs sought to harness knowledge gleaned from research to address major social problems. The Great Society initiative sought to eradicate poverty by providing better housing, education, and employment opportunities for low-income families. While ESEA has been updated a number of times since 1965, the 2001 reauthorization (NCLB) included requirements for states that are much more specific than prior versions. Specifically, NCLB puts a very heavy emphasis on evidence-based practices. For example, here is an excerpt from *No Child Left Behind: A Desktop Reference*:

> All states must submit plans to the Secretary of Education that include *evidence* that they have content and achievement standards and aligned assessments, school report card procedures, and statewide systems for holding schools and districts accountable for the achievement of their students. (U.S. Department of Education, 2002b, p. 10)

In the example above, the evidence focus is on states' assessment systems. However, it sets the stage for specifications in states' federally funded programs that require evidence-based practices. For example, among the requirements for programs to be funded under NCLB is evidence of effectiveness, which was described as "programs that have been found through scientifically based research to significantly improve the academic achievement of participating children or have strong evidence that they will achieve this result" (U.S. Department of Education, 2002b, p. 45).

In addition, language in NCLB implementation materials required that states continue to monitor student progress during program implementation. Thus, NCLB set up a set of requirements whereby states must implement evidence-based instruction and monitor student progress to verify that the programs are effective. NCLB guidance stated that:

> activities must be based on a review of scientifically based research that shows how such interventions are expected to improve student achievement. This means that there must be reliable and valid research evidence that the program activities are effective in helping teachers to improve student academic achievement. (U.S. Department of Education, 2002b, p. 53)

In contrast to earlier versions of ESEA, NCLB included numerous references to evidence-based and scientifically validated instructional practices designed to improve learning outcomes for all students. The focus on improving the performance of all students harkens back to the original focus of ESEA in 1965, when the goal was increasing performance of the poorest and most at-risk students. Greater specificity about program elements and targets for students to meet was included in certain portions of NCLB, including the Reading First, Early Reading First, and Even Start subsections.

Reading First

Thanks to the availability of excellent and conclusive research about the nature and course of reading difficulties (Foorman, 2003; Shaywitz, 2003), NCLB includes large sections specifying the exact features and components to be included in states' reading improvement programs. Specifically, states must submit evidence of how they will use evidence-based practices to teach and assess students' reading skills across the five reading domains identified by the National Reading Panel (2000). NCLB proposal guidance requires that each state

> [use] scientific evidence to enhance children's reading skills. Professional development, instructional programs, and materials used by a state education agency (SEA) or school district must focus on the five key areas that scientifically based reading research has identified as essential components of reading instruction—phonemic awareness, phonics, vocabulary, fluency, and reading comprehension. (U.S. Department of Education, 2002b, p. 24)

By having states and local school districts integrate specific reading instruction methods, the Reading First portions of NCLB focused on increasing the likelihood that students at risk for reading difficulties will receive instruction previously shown to be effective in helping such students.

Early Reading First

Another subsection of NCLB focused on evidence-based reading instruction was Early Reading First. This grant program provided funding for early childhood and kindergarten reading instruction. Again, the thrust for this program came from extensive scientific research that showed how early intervention for students identified as at risk has yielded impressive results by fostering critical prereading skills (Snow et al., 1998). For example, students as young as 3 years old were found to benefit from instruction to boost overall vocabulary knowledge.

> New research illustrates the importance of the intellectual competencies of young children and suggests specific ways to support learning through the use of strategies such as explicit and scaffolded instruction (in which adults build upon what children already know to help them accomplish a complex task by providing support where needed). An extensive body of evidence is now available stressing the importance of early reading skills, including phonological awareness and vocabulary development. Early Reading First is designed to improve these skills. (U.S. Department of Education, 2002b, p. 27)

Congress included Early Reading First in NCLB because of the persuasive evidence that early intervention works. Notably, the inclusion of early intervention in NCLB points to the importance of preventive efforts to support students in learning the precursors known to contribute to later reading development. A notable component of the Reading First and Early Reading First sections of NCLB that stands out is the way in which the legislation "requires programs to use scientifically based research to teach children cognitive and language skills. Programs must base their activities, services, and professional development on scientifically based reading research" (U.S. Department of Education, 2002b, p. 27). These criteria include emphasis on systematic, data-driven, and evidence-based practices for all levels and stages of each student's education.

Anticipating Student Needs: Prevention on Multiple Levels

The prevention orientation in NCLB follows from work done in other disciplines regarding multiple stages in program supports so that the least intrusive methods necessary are applied to support effective outcomes for all students. In particular, a three-stage prevention model common in the field of public health has been integrated into NCLB (Brown & Brown, 2005; Caplan, 1964; Doll & Haack, 2005; McCardle & Chhabra, 2004; Pressley et al., 2004). This three-stage prevention model, with primary, secondary, and tertiary components, offers a new way for educators to think about how best to help all students to be successful. According to this prevention model, programs and services designed for all students are known as primary prevention. In public health and medicine, an example of primary prevention is mandatory immunizations for certain diseases. Immunization policies were developed in the latter half of the 20th century because of scientific data documenting how vaccinating entire populations was in the general public interest (Freeman, 1994; Institute of Medicine, 2004).

Secondary prevention involves intervention for those who do not respond to the primary prevention methods. In healthcare, this includes giving flu shots to those known to be at risk for influenza due to identifiable characteristics matched to population risk factors. Individuals who are 65 or older, who have certain medical conditions, or who care for those who are ill have been shown to be much more at risk for catching the flu. Given this risk, a standard preventive health protocol involves targeting flu shots to those in the overall population who are at a greater risk for getting a bad case of the flu. Tertiary prevention includes methods and procedures for treating active cases of a disease or condition. Using the flu example, tertiary activities include the actual treatment of flu symptoms. Once a case of flu is verified, there is no sense in primary or secondary prevention, but minimizing the dangers and discomfort from the flu are in the individual's and community's best interest.

In similar ways, NCLB incorporated data from numerous studies about effective instructional practices into national education policy. Specifically, NCLB required states to develop educational programs that were based on evidence from scientific studies. In the case of reading, NCLB specifically required sequenced elements in effective reading programs for the purpose of organizing and targeting instruction to specific students at specific moments in time. As noted, this policy is grounded in a prevention model because Reading First required evidence-based reading instruction as the core curriculum for all students, but also included the requirement of increasingly more explicit and intensive instruction for those students who do not respond to the core instruction program. NCLB incorporated other examples of prevention as well. One example was the Even Start program. This program included funding for preschool education activities designed to boost the readiness of all students for kindergarten and higher-grade instruction. NCLB documentation noted that

> Even Start programs will achieve quality through new requirements to use scientifically based research evidence to design program activities, especially reading-readiness activities for preschool children. The new state indicators of program quality will allow states to make informed decisions about continuation funding for subgrantees based on whether or not they are showing sufficient progress. (U.S. Department of Education, 2002b, p. 32)

Of note, the Even Start guidelines require that states and programs document evidence of student progress. This feature of the guidelines is firmly rooted in a prevention model, because only by examining the results from primary prevention activities can one determine which individuals in a given population need secondary prevention programs.

NCLB included language related to other aspects of primary prevention as well. For example, NCLB included funding for before- and after-school programs for students whose parents work long hours. Such programming relates to primary prevention because other research has shown how students who are well supervised outside of school are more likely to achieve better school outcomes. By offering high-quality before- and after-school programs, students whose parents must work long hours to make ends meet are more likely to be as successful in school as those whose parents can take them to school and be with them as soon as school ends each day. The scientific nature of such programs must meet the same standards of evidence. For example,

> A [before- or after-school] program must be based on an objective assessment of the need for before- and after-school programs (including summer school programs) and activities in schools and communities; an established set of performance measures aimed at ensuring quality academic enrichment opportunities; and, if appropriate, scientifically based research that provides evidence that the program will help students meet state and local academic achievement standards. (U.S. Department of Education, 2002b, p. 86)

Taken as a whole, the core provisions of NCLB incorporate evidence-based practices in systematic and data driven ways that complement and match our RTI model in numerous ways.

RTI COMPONENTS IN IDEIA 2004

Additional efforts to integrate RTI with education policy were featured in the most recent reauthorization of the Individuals with Disabilities Education Improvement Act (IDEIA, 2004). Specifically, RTI language was explicitly incorporated into the legislation. Some of the impetus for including RTI language in special education policy came from the same research evidence that promoted its inclusion in NCLB. In addition to the scientific evidence for specific reading instruction methods, other data have shown a large increase in the number of students who are receiving special education services (National Center for Education Statistics, 2004). The disability for which students most commonly receive special education services is specific learning disability. Additional data further reveal that the majority of students who have been identified as learning disabled have reading problems (Swanson, Harris, & Graham, 2003). The evidence of increases in the number of students receiving special education services alongside the high number of those students having reading problems suggested that efforts to meet the needs of students with reading problems were required.

The specific language in IDEIA (2004) included three elements that integrate evidence-based practices, including (1) a requirement for the use of scientifically based reading instruction, (2) evaluation of how well a student responds to intervention, and (3) emphasis on the role of data for decision making. In essence, these three requirements are the core components of RTI. IDEIA 2004 also included language allowing school districts to make determinations about learning disabilities without using IQ scores. The IDEIA 2004 language regarding RTI for eligibility determination related to applications of RTI and will be discussed in Chapter 3. The requirement for evidence-based reading instruction practices came directly from the research literature about scientifically based methods. IDEIA 2004 specified scientifically based instruction for reading only and did not include such a requirement for math or writing instruction; this omission was attributed to the smaller amount of research on math and writing instruction.

The second RTI component found in IDEIA 2004 related to data. The law stated that the procedures for determining whether a student has a disability need to take into consideration how a student responds to good instruction. The third element specified that the decisions about a student's response to intervention have to be data-based. Taken together, the RTI language in IDEIA 2004 captured many elements seen in NCLB about evidence-based practices but added an increased emphasis on using data to inform instruction. The main thrust behind the evidence and data-based language in IDEIA 2004 came from the concern that too many students end up in special education. While special education is recognized as an important and crucial resource for students with disabilities, many educators, administrators, and policymakers have long been concerned that it is often perceived as the only mechanism by which a student can receive additional instruction and support.

EMERGING STANDARDS IN EDUCATION POLICY

Two major U.S. education policies have reshaped key aspects of how student educational progress is understood. NCLB required that teachers use instructional practices validated in scientifically based studies. IDEIA 2004 extended that requirement and stipulated that teachers collect their own data about student performance and utilize scientific methods to determine whether their own application of scientifically based practices improved outcomes for students. Notably, NCLB applies to all students, while IDEIA 2004 is activated only when a student encounters difficulties in the general education curriculum. Still, the requirement in IDEIA 2004 that data about a student's performance in the general education curriculum be utilized in order to make a determination of learning disability means that certain IDEIA policies will have an effect on general education practices. In Chapter 3 we review and discuss the specific components in IDEIA 2004 that have further expanded the application of evidence-based education practices in both general and special education.

3

RTI Instead of Discrepancy Models

RTI AND SPECIAL EDUCATION

Although RTI is a general education-based mechanism for monitoring student progress, it can also be used as part of special education decision making. In particular, RTI can be used as part of the assessment procedures to identify a learning disability (see Box 3.1). For a number of years researchers have called for a change in how students are identified with learning disabilities (LD) (Kavale, 2001). A number of reasons for changing the procedures and practices surrounding LD identification have been identified, including the lack of evidence to support the current method, evidence that other methods work just as well or better, and a desire to do away with a practice whereby students must "wait to fail" (Elliott & Fuchs, 1997; Fletcher et al., 2004; Reschly, 1997; Stanovich, 1991, 1993; Vellutino, Scanlon, & Lyon, 2000). This chapter addresses all three of these issues and presents information about how RTI procedures offer a better method for identifying students with learning disabilities.

BOX 3.1. RTI and Special Education Eligibility

RTI is not about reducing the number of students eligible for special education services. RTI is about pairing students with effective interventions and documenting student progress. If it results in fewer students receiving special education services, that's probably a good thing. Why? While special education has the goal of ensuring that all children in the United States have access to a *free appropriate public education* in the *least restrictive environment* (FAPE/LRE), it has not always achieved that goal (Kavale, 2001, 2002). RTI is about showing whether any intervention—general or special—achieves the goal of improving student outcomes.

PROBLEMS WITH IQ–ACHIEVEMENT DISCREPANCIES

The IQ–achievement discrepancy formula method for identifying LD emerged as a means of operationally defining the features associated with certain learning problems. Specifically, the presence of an average to above-average IQ along with lower-than-expected academic achievement provided a way of documenting that a student *could* learn but was *not* learning (Peterson & Shinn, 2002). Despite the apparent face validity and logic of the IQ–achievement model, many years' worth of data have shown that it does not reliably identify those students with learning disabilities (Fletcher, Morris, & Lyon, 2003; Glutting, McDermott, Watkins, Kush, & Konold, 1997; Stanovich, 2000; Spear-Swerling & Sternberg, 1996).

For example, many studies comparing different subtypes of reading difficulties have shown virtually no differences between those who were identified as having a specific reading disability and those with no disability (Spear-Swerling & Sternberg, 1996; Stanovich, 2000). In these studies, the students who were identified as having a reading disability (RD) were documented to have a significant discrepancy between their intellectual capacity or quotient (IQ) and their academic achievement. The other students, referred to as "garden-variety" poor readers, had the same types of reading problems but no discrepancy (Fuchs, Fuchs, Mathes, Lipsey, & Eaton, 2000; O'Malley, Francis, Foorman, Fletcher, & Swank, 2002; Stanovich, 1991, 2000; Vellutino et al., 2000). The studies comparing these groups have been quite consistent in finding that the presence of an IQ–achievement discrepancy neither establishes nor confirms the presence of a learning disability. Far fewer studies have been done concerning the accuracy of IQ–achievement discrepancy scores for identifying other subtypes of learning disability, such as in math or writing. A few studies have shown that the presence of a discrepancy does not automatically mean that a student is learning disabled (Graham & Harris, 1997). All of these studies have in common the finding that the nature of the intervention provided to all students is more important than the etiology or symptoms (National Association of School Psychologists, 2002).

Why Is the IQ–Achievement Equation Problematic?

Many people are shocked to learn that IQ scores are not the best indicators of ability. While there is evidence that IQs are modestly predictive of individual ability after the age of 10, they offer only limited indicators of students' abilities and potential before then (Salvia & Ysseldyke, 2004; Sattler, 2001). A number of research studies have shown that IQ is a very poor predictor of reading skill (Graham & Harris, 1997; Siegel & Himel, 1998; Stage, Jenkins, & Berninger, 2003; Stanovich, 1991, 1993; Stuebing et al., 2002; Vellutino et al., 2000). What these studies have consistently shown is that IQ, as well as IQ–achievement score discrepancies do not predict which students will have reading difficulties and which ones will benefit from additional intensive instruction (Lyon et al., 2004). If IQ scores do not help determine which students need additional instruction and which students have specific learning disabilities, there is no rationale to continue their use. Indeed, IQ scores of young children are so variable that they indicate very little about long-term abilities (Francis, 2003; Sattler, 2000).

Importantly, many of the most critical skills taught in school need to be learned well before age 10 in order to have their optimal effects (Blachman et al., 2004; Schatschneider, Francis, Carlson, Fletcher, & Foorman, 2004). For example, students who learn key reading subskills before grade 3 are very likely to be successful in school and life; conversely, those students who do not learn to read by grade 3 are very likely to remain behind for the rest of their school careers and are much more likely to drop out of school (Snow et al., 1998; Stanovich, 2000). Thus, at the very time when it is most important to know which students are struggling in school, IQ scores offer very little useful information. Tests of academic achievement are more helpful in the early grades, because they indicate the extent to which a student has mastered certain specific skills or knowledge.

It is when achievement test scores are compared with IQ scores that predictors of student abilities are most likely to get confounded (National Association of School Psychologists, 2003). As noted, IQ scores are much less reliable for young children. While achievement test scores may offer more accurate information when the two are compared, the effects of one on the other interfere. Specifically, when a student has struggled to learn certain basic skills such as reading, basic arithmetic, and spelling, he or she has probably missed out on other elements of instruction such as key content. This means that his or her general fund of knowledge and skills is likely to be lower than that of classmates who have mastered the basic academic skills (Kranzler, 1997). When tested using an IQ–achievement discrepancy, it is possible (even likely) that difficulties with basic skills will interfere with obtaining accurate estimates of the student's IQ (Siegel, 2003). In such cases, the student's IQ and achievement scores are more likely to be similar and lacking a discrepancy. Students who have no discrepancy have not been eligible for extra instruction under past special education rules. Sadly, these students have had to get really, really far behind in their academic performance before they become eligible for services. They've had to "wait to fail."

Responding Instead of Waiting

The Individuals with Disabilities Education Improvement Act passed by the U.S. Congress in November 2004 included language specifically incorporating RTI practices into special education procedures. A summary of the RTI language in IDEIA 2004 is found in Table 3.1. Sections 602 and 614 of IDEIA 2004 include language specific to RTI. Section 602 of the law includes definitions of important terms in the law, including a definition of "specific learning disability" (SLD). As shown in Table 3.1, the definition of SLD did not change from the definition found in the preceding version of IDEA (1997). Importantly, the definition still includes a reference to "basic psychological processes" as well as a variety of possible manifestations, including "the imperfect ability to listen, think, speak, read, write, spell, or do mathematical calculations." Again, as in 1997, there are important rule-out criteria in the definition such that students cannot be identified as having a specific learning disability if the "learning problem . . . is primarily the result of visual, hear-

TABLE 3.1. Sections of the Individuals with Disabilities Education Improvement Act of 2004 Related to RTI Methods

Section	Excerpt
602	(30) SPECIFIC LEARNING DISABILITY.
	(A) IN GENERAL. The term "specific learning disability" means a disorder in 1 or more of the basic psychological processes involved in understanding or in using language, spoken or written, which disorder may manifest itself in the imperfect ability to listen, think, speak, read, write, spell, or do mathematical calculations.
	(B) DISORDERS INCLUDED.—Such term includes such conditions as perceptual disabilities, brain injury, minimal brain dysfunction, dyslexia, and developmental aphasia.
	(C) DISORDERS NOT INCLUDED.—Such term does not include a learning problem that is primarily the result of visual, hearing, or motor disabilities, of mental retardation, of emotional disturbance, or of environmental, cultural, or economic disadvantage.
614	(5) SPECIAL RULE FOR ELIGIBILITY DETERMINATION. In making a determination of eligibility under paragraph (4)(A), a child shall not be determined to be a child with a disability if the determinant factor for such determination is:
	(A) lack of appropriate instruction in reading, including in the essential components of reading instruction (as defined in section 1208(3) of the Elementary and Secondary Education Act of 1965);
	(B) lack of instruction in math; or
	(C) limited English proficiency.
	(6) SPECIFIC LEARNING DISABILITIES.
	(A) IN GENERAL. Notwithstanding section 607(b), when determining whether a child has a specific learning disability as defined in section 602, a local educational agency shall not be required to take into consideration whether a child has a severe discrepancy between achievement and intellectual ability in oral expression, listening comprehension, written expression, basic reading skill, reading comprehension, mathematical calculation, or mathematical reasoning.
	(B) ADDITIONAL AUTHORITY.—In determining whether a child has a specific learning disability, a local educational agency may use a process that determines if the child responds to scientific, research-based intervention as a part of the evaluation procedures described in paragraphs (2) and (3).

ing, or motor disabilities, of mental retardation, of emotional disturbance, or of environmental, cultural, or economic disadvantage." Thus, the core definition of SLD in IDEIA 2004 remains unchanged from its predecessors.

What is different in IDEIA 2004 is the language found in section 614 of the law. Section 614 covers the evaluation procedures allowable for special education eligibility. Items 5 and 6 of section 614 include language specifically related to RTI practices. Item 5 of this section provides additional clarification about the conditions under which a determination of SLD would be inappropriate due to lack of instruction. Here, the law specifies that "a child shall not be determined to be a child with a disability if the determinant factor for such determination is . . . lack of appropriate instruction in reading, including in the essential components of reading instruction (as defined in section 1208(3) of the Elementary and Secondary Education Act [ESEA] of 1965)." The text goes on to make a similar requirement for both math and writing instruction. Of note, IDEIA 2004 requires the "essential components of reading instruction" only and not for math or writing. Here, it is important to know that the reference to the ESEA refers to the current version of that act, which is NCLB. *What this means is that IDEIA 2004 references NCLB in stating that students cannot be found eligible as students with specific learning disabilities if they have not received scientifically based instruction, which, in the case of reading, includes the five components of reading included in NCLB.*

The next part of section 614 of IDEIA 2004 includes language specifically related to evaluation for SLD. Part 6 (titled "Specific Learning Disabilities") removes the requirement that an IQ–achievement discrepancy must be used to identify SLD. Specifically, part 6(A) states that "a local educational agency *shall not* be required to take into consideration whether a child has a severe discrepancy between achievement and intellectual ability in oral expression, listening comprehension, written expression, basic reading skill, reading comprehension, mathematical calculation, or mathematical reasoning." This is a dramatic and important shift from earlier versions of IDEIA, which focused on the use of the IQ–achievement discrepancy as the means for determining the presence of SLD.

Part 6(B), also specifically related to SLD, adds additional information about the procedures that may be used to identify learning disabilities. This next part integrates language from part 5 on scientifically based instruction with RTI procedures by stating that "in determining whether a child has a specific learning disability, a local educational agency may use a process that determines if the child *responds* to scientific, research-based *intervention* as a part of the evaluation procedures." Here, the law allows for the use of RTI procedures as part of special education eligibility procedures. In combination, parts 5 and 6 of section 614 of IDEIA 2004 create a new mechanism for how students with learning disabilities are identified. By requiring scientifically based instruction as a prerequisite for evaluation, and by including RTI methods as allowable assessment procedures, IDEIA 2004 makes a significant commitment to utilizing data-driven decision making for all students. This new language also includes a more specific bridge between general and special education by referencing NCLB requirements in the law. In doing so, lawmakers have made clear the requirement that all branches and components of public education—general and specialized—use and report on data-based instructional practices.

EMPIRICAL SUPPORT FOR RTI IN SPECIAL EDUCATION PRACTICE

A few studies have investigated the efficacy of RTI methods in special education. In a longitudinal study of RTI methods, Case, Speece, and Malloy (2003) found that RTI methods identified students as well as or better than discrepancy methods of identification. The student features used to distinguish which students had reading disabilities were consistent over the time that the students were in the study. A study by Fletcher et al. (2002) yielded similar results. Marston, Muyskens, Lau, and Canter (2003) reported similar robust findings from data collected longitudinally in the Minneapolis public schools. Importantly, these three studies focused on differentiating students with and without disabilities.

The usefulness of RTI methods in identifying degrees of need among students and reducing the number of students receiving intensive services has been documented as well. O'Connor (2003) reported that RTI procedures are particularly helpful in identifying students with learning difficulties in the early primary grades. Such use of RTI enables teachers to determine which students need intensive services as early as first grade so that supports can be provided as quickly as possible. Many students whose learning difficulties were identified in first grade were able to be successful in third grade with much less intensive supports than expected. In similar research Tilly (2003) found that RTI practices are consistent with primary prevention activities as much as early intervention. By using RTI with preschoolers, teachers were able to prevent some special education placements altogether.

While much of the research on RTI has focused on very young children, some researchers have looked at the implications for older students. Torgeson (2003) reported that RTI methods hold promise for students in upper elementary school because they can provide high-quality instruction to students in a rapid and data-driven way. For example, Torgeson and his colleagues found that RTI procedures helped third-grade students improve their reading skills in significant ways. For those students still struggling at the end of the intervention, the data collected as part of RTI were useful for suggesting the next steps in the assessment process. When used in conjunction with other assessment methods, RTI procedures can facilitate the most precise assessment of students' learning needs (Semrud-Clikeman, 2003). It is noteworthy that the National Joint Committee on Learning Disabilities endorsed the RTI approach to LD identification as a better way to support students' learning needs (National Joint Committee on Learning Disabilities, 2002).

RTI AS PART OF SPECIAL EDUCATION

As noted, the RTI language in IDEIA 2004 was included for the purpose of helping to determine which students are eligible for special education. When RTI procedures are used after an eligibility determination is made, they are incorporated into the IEP. For example, a student who is struggling with learning math facts despite the use of a scientifically validated general education math program (Tier 1) would be provided with a Tier 2 intervention such as small-group instruction in basic math facts. Such instruction would be in addition to the general education instruction. While the Tier 2 intervention is being used, regular (at least weekly) data on the student's progress would be collected. Such data could include weekly 2-minute curriculum-based measures of the computation skills being taught. If the student did not show progress over a period of time (i.e., 3 weeks), another, perhaps more intensive, Tier 2 intervention could be tried. After 3 more weeks, the student's progress data would again be reviewed. If those data indicated there was still a lack of progress in learning the computation facts, then a referral for a comprehensive evaluation would be made.

Importantly, referral for an evaluation does not guarantee that the student will be found eligible for special education. The referral and assessment process includes a comprehensive evaluation of the student's school history and current performance. The data collected during both Tiers 1 and 2 need to be included in the comprehensive evaluation. These data document the implementation of scientifically based instruction, as required by NCLB and IDEA 2004. Additional testing also needs to be conducted. The other assessments should provide information about cognitive processes and basic competencies not documented with the RTI data. In the earlier cited case of math computation difficulties, the additional assessment would be likely to include tests of memory skills to see whether the student has a core difficulty holding numbers in memory while trying to add, subtract, multiply, or divide them. If the comprehensive evaluation findings show that the student has a persistent difficulty with both expected academic tasks (e.g., math computation) and one or more of the underlying cognitive processes that are needed to perform such tasks, then identification of a learning disability is made.

SUMMARY

IDEIA 2004 includes new provisions specifically incorporating RTI policies and procedures. By including language that calls for scientifically based instruction in reading and math as a prerequisite for identification of a specific learning disability, IDEIA 2004 includes an expectation that Tier 1 RTI procedures will be used. The special language in IDEIA 2004 that allows RTI Tier 2 procedures to be used as part of the process by which a student is identified as having a learning disability allows schools to put in place systematic intervention procedures for addressing students' learning needs as soon as they are identified by a classroom teacher and confirmed with supporting data. These elements are a critical bridge between general and special education and build on the language in NCLB that calls for high standards and outcomes for all students, including those with disabilities. Chapter 4 will provide both definition and discussion of what constitutes evidence-based instruction, a key underpinning of both NCLB and IDEIA 2004. Chapter 5 will cover single-subject research designs and how they can be used to collect data about student progress and document the efficacy of specific interventions. Numerous examples of each RTI step will be included in Chapters 6 through 9.

4

Evidence-Based Interventions

Over the past several years the educational research literature has increasingly emphasized the importance of making sure that interventions being implemented with students in school settings are empirically based. For example, the journal *School Psychology Quarterly (SPQ)* devoted an entire issue (Vol. 17, No. 4; 14 articles) to a thorough discussion of evidence-based interventions. The authors of the special *SPQ* issue reviewed and discussed the results obtained by the Task Force on Evidence-Based Interventions in School Psychology, which was founded and supported in 1999 by both the Division of School Psychology of the American Psychological Association (APA) and the Society for the Study of School Psychology (Gutkin, 2002). At the core of these articles is a belief that school psychologists and other school-based professionals have a professional responsibility for both promoting and implementing interventions that are evidence-based as well as objectively evaluating the effectiveness of those interventions.

Lest one think that this emerging emphasis on evidence-based practices is limited to national task forces and academic circles, one only needs to review professional standards and ethics to find numerous references to evidence-based interventions. For example, review of the National Association of School Psychologists (NASP) *Professional Conduct Manual: Principles for Professional Ethics* and *Guidelines for the Provision of School Psychological Services* (2000) discloses several professional practice standards stating that school psychologists have an obligation to implement empirically based interventions, to use a data-based decision-making process to monitor and modify interventions, and to collect data to evaluate the efficacy of interventions. For example:

C. *Assessment and Intervention*

    C4: School psychologists use assessment techniques, counseling and therapy procedures, consultation techniques, and other direct and indirect service methods that the profession considers to be responsible, *research-based* practice.

    C6: School psychologists develop interventions that are appropriate to the presenting problems and are consistent with *data* collected. They modify or terminate the treatment plan when the *data* indicate the plan is not achieving desired goals. (NASP, 2000; emphasis added)

In addition some of the NASP practice guidelines specify that evidence-based practices are expected:

Practice Guideline 1

School psychologists use a decision-making process in collaboration with other team members to (a) identify academic and behavior problems, (b) collect and analyze information to understand the problems, (c) make decisions about service delivery, and (d) evaluate the outcomes of the service delivery.

   School psychologists must (a) utilize current professional literature on various aspects of education and child development, (b) translate *research* into practice through the problem-solving process, and (c) use *research* design and statistics to conduct investigations to develop and facilitate effective services.

   1.1 School psychologists define problems in ways that (a) identify desired goals (e.g., academic/behavioral), (b) are measurable, (c) are agreed upon by those involved, and (d) are linked appropriately to assessment strategies.

   1.3 School psychologists develop and implement effective interventions that are based upon the *data* collected and related directly to the desired outcomes of those interventions.

   1.4 School psychologists use appropriate assessment information to evaluate interventions to determine their effectiveness, their need for modification, or their need for redevelopment. Effectiveness is determined by the relationship between the actual outcome of the intervention and the desired goal articulated in the problem solving process. (NASP, 2000, pp. 40–41; emphasis added)

NASP's Practice Guideline 1 makes it clear that school psychology professionals are expected to use research evidence in all aspects of decision making. Similarly, Practice Guideline 3 sets a clear expectation for setting goals for students and monitoring goal attainment:

Practice Guideline 3

School psychologists (in collaboration with others) develop challenging but achievable cognitive and academic goals for all students, provide information about ways on which students can achieve these goals, and monitor student progress toward these goals.

   3.1 School psychologists apply current empirically based theory and knowledge of learning theory and cognitive processes to the development of *effective instructional strategies* to promote student learning and social and emotional development.

   3.4 School psychologists assist in facilitating and implementing a variety of *research-based* instructional methods (e.g., cooperative learning, class-wide peer tutoring, cognitive strategy training) to enhance learning of students at the individual, group, and system level.

   3.7 School psychologists are informed about advances in curriculum and instruction and share this knowledge with educators, parents, and the community at large to promote improvement in instruction, student achievement, and healthy lifestyles. (NASP, 2000, pp. 43–44; emphasis added)

Again, as in Guideline 1, research is included many times and sets a standard that all activities will revolve around evidence. Also present in Guideline 3 is the standard that instructional programs will be monitored while being implemented and student progress reviewed. These standards allow for a variety of theoretical and empirical perspectives, so long as they are scientifically based.

Practice Guideline 4

School psychologists make decisions based on multiple theoretical perspectives and translate current *scientific information* to develop effective behavioral, affective, or adaptive goals for all students, facilitate the implementation of programs/interventions to achieve these goals, and monitor progress toward these goals.

> 4.1 School psychologists use decision-making models (e.g., functional behavioral assessment) that consider the antecedents, consequences, functions, and potential causes of behavioral problems experienced by students with disabilities, which may impair learning or socialization. (NASP, 2000, p. 44; emphasis added)

School-based practitioners may find themselves conflicted when these ethical principles and standards conflict with the practice of school psychology within educational settings.

Consider the following example. A school psychologist is a member of a student assistance team (SAT) that also includes the principal, regular education teacher, special education teacher, speech pathologist, social worker, and occupational therapist. The SAT meets on a weekly basis to review and discuss the needs of specific students (assessments, goals/objectives interventions, positive behavior support plans, etc.). During discussions of a student who has a long history of attention deficits and excess motor behaviors (e.g., fidgeting in seat, pencil tapping, rocking in seat, etc.), a team member recommended the possibility of using a procedure that she heard about during a professional conference. She described a procedure in which the student would be directed to listen to audiotapes featuring recordings of environmental sounds (e.g., ocean waves, bird calls, whales, among others). She explained that the student's excess motor behavior was his way of seeking out environmental stimulation, stating that he was "environmentally starved." She hypothesized that audiotapes of environmental sounds would address his unmet needs, providing him with a "diet" of environmental input that would result in a *decrease* in excess motor behaviors and a concomitant *increase* in attending during instruction. She went on to report that this intervention had potential for increasing the reading skills of students with learning disabilities. She explained that the intervention would be particularly effective with students who have difficulties with reading comprehension because listening to the environmentally enriched audiotapes would provide them with sensory input that would stimulate a groundswell of contextual cues, resulting in a direct connection between words in print and environmentally laden visual imagery. She explained that, for the procedure that to be effective, the student should (1) wear headphones to listen to the audiotapes, (2) be seated in a quiet and preferably isolated setting, and (3) listen to the audiotapes for 15 minutes at least 3 times per school day.

The reaction of team members was mixed, ranging from complete enthusiasm for this novel approach to outright skepticism. Given her solid grounding in NASP ethical principles and standards, the school psychologist stated that she was unfamiliar with this intervention and asked if there was a research base supporting its use in treatment of attention deficits and reading comprehension in elementary-level students. The colleague endorsing the intervention explained that she had learned about the intervention at a presentation at the conference from a "very credible professor" from _____ University (a well-known university on the West Coast). She explained that the presentation included videotapes of students listening to the environmental audiotapes, and in each case the students were sitting quietly and were very attentive. She also explained that the presenter reported several cases of students who experienced gains in reading comprehension for as long as 3 years after exposure to the audiotapes. Several team members indicated that, given the current student's long history of attention deficits, this intervention might "be worth a try," adding that "we have nothing to lose." Several team members discussed trying this intervention with students who have reading disorders.

Faced with this dilemma, what should an educator do? Our professional ethics and standards mandate that interventions be evidence-based. How do we maintain our commitment to our professional ideals in situations when these ideals are compromised? Other questions to consider that are related to this quandary are:

- What's the rationale for requiring an evidence base for interventions?
- What constitutes evidence?
- Do anecdotal reports, subjective opinions, or testimonials constitute evidence?
- What do we do in those situations in which novel interventions are recommended, but our review of the literature does not identify a solid research base?

Read on. The remaining sections of this chapter will answer these questions and provide the reader with a model for documenting the degree to which interventions are evidence-based.

WHAT IS THE RATIONALE FOR REQUIRING AN EVIDENCE BASE FOR INTERVENTIONS?

First of all, it's the right thing to do. Using interventions that have a proven track record *increases the probability* of positive outcomes for students. Notice that we did not use the term *guarantee*. We all know that in the schools there are very few guarantees, and when it comes to interventions, *guaranteeing* their efficacy is foolhardy. Just because an intervention was shown to be effective with a group of students with learning disabilities in Portland, Maine, and later found to be equally effective with a group of students with emotional disabilities in Waterloo, Iowa, there are no guarantees that the same intervention will be effective with the student population you are serving. However, when we select interventions that have a solid research base, provide the necessary resources to implement the intervention with precision, and collect meaningful data documenting student progress, we have greatly increased the chances of effecting positive student behavior change (Foorman, Breier, & Fletcher, 2003).

BOX 4.1. Facilitated Communication:
The Intervention Cart before the Research Horse

During the early 1990s a new strategy for enabling persons with severe disabilities to communicate their needs swept the country. Facilitated communication was a method in which a "facilitator" (e.g., parent, teacher, therapist) provided physical assistance to support a person with a disability in his or her pointing to a keyboard (or laminated copy of a keyboard) and spelling out words and sentences. In its infancy of implementation within the United States, facilitated communication (FC) appeared to be a revolutionary procedure that would significantly enhance the communication skills and quality of life of thousands of persons with disabilities.

In our own experiences we witnessed numerous cases in which individuals identified with autism spectrum disorders, persons with cerebral palsy, and students with severe developmental disabilities who had significant expressive language delays were exposed to FC and were *reported* to demonstrate immediate and significant improvements in their ability to communicate. In some cases, individuals who were previously viewed as "untestable" were evaluated with a facilitator using FC procedures and scored in the average to above-average ranges on measures of academic and cognitive performance. In short order, daylong workshops and trainings began popping up across the country, and FC began to be used in schools, homes, agencies, and institutions. Amazing success stories were being reported. This appeared to be a life-altering intervention. Next came objective research.

Data from numerous studies showed that persons with disabilities were not directing their motions and that FC was not a consistent or reliable method of communication for persons with disabilities. Based on their reviews of this emerging empirical evidence, numerous professional organizations issued position statements that FC was invalid. For example, in 1993 the American Academy of Child and Adolescent Psychiatry (AACAP) stated that "studies have repeatedly demonstrated that FC is not a scientifically valid technique for individuals with autism or mental retardation." In 1994 the American Psychological Association, after review of numerous empirical studies, concluded their position statement by stating, "Therefore, be it resolved that APA adopts the position that facilitated communication is a controversial and unproved communicative procedure with no scientifically demonstrated support for its efficacy." This was followed by comparable position statements from the American Speech–Language–Hearing Association (1994), the American Association on Mental Retardation (2005), the Association for Behavior Analysis (1995), and the American Academy of Pediatrics (1998).

By that time, however, countless numbers of persons with disabilities had been exposed to invalid interventions incorporating FC, and their families had been offered false promises. Thousands of taxpayer dollars and uncounted hours had been spent in using FC *instead* of safe, effective, and validated methods for teaching persons with developmental disabilities to communicate for themselves (Foxx, 1999). Clearly, in the case of FC the intervention cart raced way ahead of the research horse.

Second, interventions based only on theories, professional opinions, testimonials, and subjective evaluation, when subsequently evaluated empirically, have often been shown to be ineffective. Consider the case of facilitated communication (FC). FC is a procedure in which a facilitator (e.g., teacher, parent, educational technician) provides physical support that enables a person with disabilities to type on a keyboard (or to point to a photocopied and laminated keyboard). Supporters of FC believed that this method increased the expressive communication skills of persons with disabilities. Based on theory and anecdotal reports, in the early 1990s its use was widely recommended by numerous academics and practitioners (e.g., school psychologists, speech pathologists, special educators, etc.). This intervention swept the country and was implemented within schools with students with a wide range of disabilities including cerebral palsy, Down syndrome, and autistic disorder, among others. When evaluated scientifically, this intervention was not found to have an empirical basis. In short, it was found to be an unreliable means of communication for students with disabilities (see Box 4.1 on FC for additional information).

Third, continued implementation of ineffective interventions results in the lack of progress and delays the implementation of effective interventions. If an intervention does not result in positive outcomes for the student, then it is time to move on and employ interventions that are effective. Students and their families have the right to expect that school practitioners will only implement interventions that have a high probability of being successful. Moreover, students and their families have the right to expect that interventions will be implemented with precision (see Box 4.2) and that objective documentation will demonstrate student progress.

BOX 4.2. Treatment Integrity

We can talk all day long about designing assessment-based, student-focused, and evidence-based interventions. However, if the intervention is *not* implemented correctly and consistently, then (1) student progress and (2) our ability to determine the efficacy of the intervention are both severely compromised. Treatment integrity refers to the degree to which an intervention is implemented as designed. There are several ways of increasing treatment integrity. First, adopting a collaborative problem-solving approach to service delivery increases team members' acceptance and understanding of interventions. Second, providing all interventionists with training in the implementation of interventions and in data-recording procedures is also important. The use of direct instruction and performance feedback (coaching) represents a best-practices model of training. Third, providing ongoing feedback and support during the implementation phase cannot be neglected. This involves conducting reliability checks in which a team member observes the interventionist's implementation of the intervention and (1) records the degree of accuracy of implementation of the components of the intervention and (2) simultaneously but independently records outcome data. This permits an analysis of the degree with which the treatment is implemented precisely as intended and interobserver agreement concerning the occurrence of target behaviors.

DO ANECDOTAL REPORTS, SUBJECTIVE OPINIONS, OR TESTIMONIALS CONSTITUTE EVIDENCE?

Our media abound with instances of infomercials and advertisements proclaiming incredible treatment gains (or losses in the case of weight management products). While replete with testimonials espousing magnificent improvements, these interventions often do not have a solid research base objectively documenting their efficacy (see Box 4.3). Most all of us can recall situations in which a family member, friend, or colleague reported the *personal* benefits of a particular intervention (e.g., diet, herbal treatment, exercise equipment, etc.). Testimonials are in and of themselves subjective and biased and therefore are not objective documentation of the effectiveness of the intervention. Likewise, a colleague may report perceived benefits of a particular intervention with a group of students. Without objective documentation, such opinions are not objective forms of evidence. Opinions are not proof. Testimonials are not objective. However, although not objective forms of evidence, these opinions are not valueless. Rather, from a

---

BOX 4.3. Pseudoscience, Nonscience, and Nonsense

School-based practitioners are bombarded with recommendations for interventions. Some are evidence-based, but many of these recommended interventions and are *not* grounded in science or any form of objective analysis. For example, in our careers in school settings we have been confronted with recommended strategies to improve academic performance such as megavitamin therapy, sensory integration, optical training, auditory training, and guided reading without direct exposure to print, among others. We refer to those interventions that do not have a solid empirical basis as falling within the categories of pseudoscience, nonscience, and nonsense.

PSEUDOSCIENCE

Pseudoscience refers to those interventions that do not have a scientific basis but are "dressed up" to superficially resemble science (Green, 1996). Pseudoscience often involves the use of scientific jargon (e.g., "statistically significant," "proven by years of research and study") or endorsements by persons with scientific credentials to promote the efficacy of the intervention. A twist to the pseudoscience phenomenon is when previously efficacious interventions are generalized to the treatment of behaviors for which there has been no documented efficacy (e.g., the use of psychostimulants to treat reading disorders). While psychostimulants have been found to be effective in increasing sustained attention, there is no objective evidence that these medications directly increase reading skills. These medications may increase reading performance (e.g., increased reading comprehension due to higher levels of on-task behavior during reading), but reading skills (e.g., decoding) are not enhanced by medications.

(continued)

NONSCIENCE

Nonscience is the category that includes those interventions that have no empirical basis whatsoever. These are the interventions that are based solely on testimonials, typically from persons who have no scientific background. Often based on personal experiences and subjective opinion, these interventions are on the same level of science as urban myths. You've heard the refrain "I have this cousin in Vancouver, and she found that providing her son with megadosages of vitamin C lead to a significant increases in reading skills . . . maybe we should try that with David" (the referred student with a history of reading disorders).

NONSENSE

Nonsense refers to the category in which the intervention itself, while often highly creative, has no real face validity and when subjected to sound critical thinking is regarded as being benign at best, somewhat unorthodox, leaning toward the sublime and ridiculous, and in the worst-case scenario as being neglectful or dangerous. These interventions are typically paired with extraordinary claims espousing immediate and significant improvements in behavior. For example, recently we were presented with a case involving a preschool-age child who had a history of primary enuresis (i.e., she was not completely toilet-trained). A therapist had recommended and the preschool team had subsequently implemented a sensory integration intervention that was designed to result in independent toileting behavior. The intervention involved scheduled toileting (an evidence-based component in which children are prompted to use the bathroom at prespecified times or intervals) and a procedure in which preschool staff used wooden skewers with foam balls attached to drum (i.e., a drumroll . . . rat-a-tat-tat . . .) on the top of the head of the student as he or she sat on the potty chair. The procedure involved lightly drumming on the top of his or her head to "stimulate the need to urinate" and was delivered until the student urinated, at which point the drumming was immediately halted. The therapist reported that it was a very effective intervention, because each time it was used the student urinated. In this case, further assessment revealed that after 17 weeks of intervention the student had not once self-initiated the use of a toilet to urinate and continued to experience wetting accidents on a daily basis. When provided with an evidenced-based toilet-training intervention (e.g., Steege, 1997), the student became completely toilet-trained (i.e., self-initiated and no daytime accidents) within 3 days, with only occasional nocturnal enuresis.

scientist-practitioner perspective, these ideas can be considered to be hypotheses, ones that can be tested using sound experimental procedures. When subjected to scientific examination and if supported by sound data, these hypotheses (ideas and opinions) may be found to be valid.

WHAT CONSTITUTES EVIDENCE?

Interventions evaluated with sound experimental designs that result in socially significant behavior change constitute evidence. A sound experimental design includes the following characteristics:

- Clearly defined independent variable(s) (i.e., intervention).
- Clearly defined dependent variable(s) (i.e., data).
- A set of procedures to consistently implement the independent variable.
- Procedures for accurately measuring the dependent variable.
- A design that controls for threats to the internal validity of the study.

Based on a report from the American Psychological Association's Committee on Science and Practice (Weisz & Hawley, 1999), Kratochwill and Stoiber co-chaired a task force on evidence-based interventions sponsored by Division 16 of the APA and the Society for the Study of School Psychology (Kratochwill & Stoiber, 2002; Task Force on Evidence-Based Interventions in School Psychology, 2003). This task force has offered a set of criteria for classifying interventions as being empirically supported. The task force grouped school-based interventions into five intervention/prevention content focus areas: (1) school- and community-based intervention programs for social and behavioral problems, (2) academic intervention programs, (3) family and parent intervention programs, (4) schoolwide and classroom-based programs, and (5) comprehensive and coordinated school health services (Kratochwill & Stoiber, 2002; Task Force on Evidence-Based Interventions in School Psychology, 2003).

In order to identify the research evidence for selected interventions, the task force created coding criteria for reviewing studies. The coding criteria were organized into four research methodology types: (1) between-group research, (2) single-participant research, (3) qualitative research procedures, and (4) confirmatory program evaluation (Kratochwill & Stoiber, 2002; Task Force on Evidence-Based Interventions in School Psychology, 2003). A graphic representing the model used for coding studies is found in Figure 4.1. As a result of the task force's application of the model to specific studies and data, it was decided to incorporate the qualitative research procedures and confirmatory program evaluation methods into the between-group and single-participant research methods categories. After reviewing the coding model and using it on a trial basis with a number of studies, the task force created a coding manual for identifying whether a proposed intervention has sufficient empirical support to be called evidence-based. The full text of the task force's report and *Procedural and Coding Manual for Review of Evidence-Based Interventions* can be found at www.sp-ebi.org/_workingfiles/EBImanual1.pdf.

Methodological focus	Intervention/prevention content focus				
	School- and community-based intervention program for social and behavioral problems	Academic intervention programs	Family and parent intervention programs	Schoolwide and classroom-based intervention programs	Comprehensive and coordinated school health services intervention programs
Between-group research					
Single-participant research					
Qualitative research procedures					
Confirmatory program evaluation					

The qualitative and confirmatory program criteria have been integrated into the group and single-participant manuals.

FIGURE 4.1. Organization of the Task Force *Procedural and Coding Manual* by content and methodological domains. Adapted from Kratochwill and Stoiber (2002, p. 350). Copyright 2002 by The Guilford Press. Adapted by permission.

Currently, the Task Force is involved in three efforts. The first is that the *Procedural and Coding Manual* is being revised with additional coding criteria, which will continue to offer researchers an opportunity to code intervention research along the criteria specified in the manual. Second, the Task Force has, and will continue to, distribute the *Procedural and Coding Manual* as a framework for teaching intervention research methodology courses in graduate training programs in school psychology and related fields. It is anticipated that the manual will facilitate consideration of the variety of research criteria as applied to the design of intervention research in education. Third, with the assistance of an Evidence-Based Practice Committee, the Task Force has created a new initiative to develop strategies to facilitate the integration of evidence-based prevention and intervention programs into school-based practices. The committee has met several times and is developing a form plan in concert with three national school psychology organizations to embrace this agenda for educators.

The manual includes specific coding criteria for studies that take into account the research design, participants, setting, outcomes, and internal/external validity criteria. Using a 4-point Likert-type scale, the task force identified nine key features of intervention studies to be coded. These nine features are (1) measurement, (2) comparison group, (3) primary/secondary outcomes significant, (4) educational/clinical significance, (5) durability of effects, (6) identifiable intervention components, (7) implementation fidelity, (8) replication, and (9) school- or field-based site (see Table 4.1). According to the *Manual*, for an intervention to qualify as being evidence-based, it must have been validated by one (or more) between-group or single-participant experimental design studies and meet certain minimum ratings on all nine of the enumerated features.

With *between-group experimental designs*, participants are randomly assigned to either an experimental or control group. The results of the study must show that the members of the experimental group outperformed the members of the control group based on an objective measurement of performance. Single-case experimental design (see Chapter 5 for a complete discussion and examples) may involve one subject (*n* of 1)

TABLE 4.1. Criteria for Documenting the Efficacy of Interventions

Feature	Strong evidence/ support	Promising evidence/ support	Marginal or weak evidence/ support	No evidence/ support
1. Measurement	3	2	1	0
2. Comparison group	3	2	1	0
3. Primary/secondary outcomes significant	3	2	1	0
4. Educational/clinical significance	3	2	1	0
5. Durability of effects	3	2	1	0
6. Identifiable intervention components	3	2	1	0
7. Implementation fidelity	3	2	1	0
8. Replication	3	2	1	0
9. School- or field-based site	3	2	1	0

or a small group of participants. In contrast to the situation in between-group designs, participants are not assigned to experimental or control groups. Rather, each participant experiences the intervention with his or her behavior (dependent variables) measured before, during, and after the implementation of the intervention. An intervention is found to be effective when behavior change occurs during the presentation of the intervention condition but remains stable during the baseline (no-treatment) conditions.

EMPIRICAL VALIDATION IN SCHOOL SETTINGS

In those situations in which novel interventions are recommended (i.e., thorough review of the literature does not identify a research base documenting its efficacy), school-based professionals face choices. Essentially one is left with two choices in these situations. One could simply decide that since there is not adequate empirical evidence to support the use of the intervention, then it should not be used with students—end of story. Or, alternatively, one could decide that the intervention likely has merit and hypothesize that it could have beneficial outcomes. In this case we suggest that you go with the old adage that "extraordinary claims require extraordinary proof." In short, in the absence of a solid research base, one must create one. And, of course, that means conducting a research study. "Oh, no!" you say. "Are Rachel and Mark suggesting another thesis or dissertation?" Perhaps but not necessarily. What we are suggesting is that if one is to go the route of implementing what constitutes an experimental trial, then one should use basic experimental methodologies to examine objectively the efficacy of the intervention. Most practitioners do not have the time or resources to conduct between-group studies with large groups of randomly assigned students. However, in our experience applications of novel interventions usually involve one student or a small group of students. In those cases, single-subject experimental design methodologies fit the bill quite nicely. We will discuss and provide examples of single-case designs in the next chapter.

A CAUTIONARY NOTE ABOUT EVIDENCE

Thus far we have talked about the importance of identifying a body of evidence that supports the efficacy of interventions. While an intervention may be sound empirically, it may not be applicable to all students. One of the responsibilities associated with identifying an evidence base involves knowing how to interpret the evidence. A series of solid studies consistently documenting the efficacy of a particular intervention may prove to be the base supporting an intervention with one group of students but not another group. Thus, while a study may have sound *internal validity* (i.e., the study minimized errors and controlled for potential extraneous variables), it may have limited *external validity* (i.e., limited generalizability across populations of students).

When one considers external validity, one asks such questions as "What relevance do these findings have outside the confines of the experiment?" and "To what student populations and settings are these findings applicable?" As mentioned previously, just because the study was effective with a group of students with learning disabilities in Portland, Maine, does not mean that the identical intervention will be *applicable to* and *effective with* a group of students with learning disabilities in Waterloo, Iowa. Moreover, the results of a study using single-subject experimental methodology with three students with developmental disabilities may not be an adequate base of evidence on which to build an intervention with students with emotional disability.

An old research adage continues to apply today, namely, "A limitation of between-group designs is its generalizability to individual cases, and a limitation of single-subject design methodology is its limited generalizability to groups of individuals." Statistically significant findings from between-group research might tell us that, *on average*, the experimental group outperformed the control group. But that would not guarantee that all individuals did or will show benefit if the intervention is used with them. Similarly, a single-subject design might demonstrate treatment gains with the individual but would not guarantee that the intervention will be successful beyond the limited subject pool.

When it comes to identifying interventions for individuals or small groups of students, it is important to recognize that the selection of intervention(s) needs to consider the empirical base as well as the applicability of the intervention to the student(s). In many cases, interventions prove to be person-specific based on the unique characteristics of the student, his or her learning history, and his or her response to previously implemented interventions. As school professionals operating within a problem-solving model of service delivery, our job is to conduct sound assessments, identify those unique characteristics of the student, and select interventions that are matched to the learning needs of the particular student involved.

SUMMARY

An intervention is said to be evidence-based when it has been found to be effective in cases of well-designed and robustly implemented experimental analysis. Practitioners need to be good consumers of published research. They need to read published studies with a critical eye to determine (1) whether the experimenters used sound research methodology and (2) whether the procedures employed are applicable to *your* population of students. In most cases we advocate a two-phase process of employing evidence-based interventions. Phase 1 involves conducting a literature review to identify relevant articles that support the intervention. At this point one reads the articles with a critical eye, examining both the internal and external validity of the study. Phase 2 involves the implementation and objective evaluation of the intervention, using single-subject experimental design methodology. Thus, our body of evidence consists of (1) previously conducted research that supports the intervention and (2) a current research base that documents the effectiveness of the intervention on a case-by-case basis. Next we will outline the process of documenting the efficacy of interventions with specific students.

5

Single-Subject Experimental Design

School-based practitioners have the dual responsibility of conducting meaningful assessments that lead to the design of effective interventions and objectively evaluating the effectiveness of those interventions. In this chapter we describe how single-subject experimental design methodology is used within a problem-solving approach to assess student behavior and to evaluate the efficacy of interventions.

Single-subject experimental design methodologies are critical components in both the assessment and intervention phases of a problem-solving model of school psychology practice (Berg, Wacker, & Steege, 1995; Polaha & Allen, 1999; Steege et al., 2002; Steege & Wacker, 1995). Single-subject experimental design methodology is based on a hypothesis-testing approach in which specific designs are used to test specific hypotheses. For example, functional analysis procedures typically utilize either a reversal or alternating treatments design to compare the influence of such variables as contingent social attention, removal of instructional stimuli, and tangible reinforcers (e.g., candy or toys) on the occurrence of specific target behaviors. Alternating treatments designs are also used to compare the relative effectiveness of two or more interventions, thus serving both an assessment and evaluation purpose. Case study (AB), reversal (ABAB), or multiple-baseline designs are most often used during the implementation phase to evaluate the efficacy of the intervention.

Unlike between-group designs, which include experimental and control groups, single-subject experimental designs involve the evaluation of a single person or small group before, during, and following the implementation of the intervention. Single-subject experimental designs control for threats to the internal validity of a study by:

- Establishing a baseline measure (dependent variable) of student behavior or academic performance.
- Introducing an intervention (independent variable).
- Documenting the effects of the intervention through repeated measurement.
- Either withdrawing and reintroducing the intervention and studying its effects or repeating the baseline and intervention phases.

When the implementation and withdrawal of the intervention result in behavior change, a functional relationship between the independent variable (intervention) and dependent variable (measures of behavior/performance) is demonstrated. Or, when the student's behavior change is replicated during the intervention phase only, one can be certain that the intervention is responsible for changes in student behavior. With single-case experimental designs, replication is demonstrated with the student across settings (e.g., math and science classes; home and school), behaviors (e.g., math worksheets and science homework), and personnel (e.g., special education teacher, mainstream teacher) (Steege et al., 2002).

Polaha and Allen (1999) and Steege et al. (2002) identified a number of reasons why single-case experimental designs are a best-practices method for evaluating the effectiveness of interventions, including:

1. Objective documentation of student progress is demonstrated.
2. Ongoing interventions allow the team to quickly identify effective and ineffective components and make necessary adjustments to the interventions (i.e., data-based decision making).
3. Practitioners have an ethical responsibility to evaluate the efficacy of interventions and single-subject experimental designs.
4. Federal, state, and agency regulations require documentation of intervention effectiveness.
5. Such interventions are applicable to and easy to use with individuals and small groups.

Additionally, single-subject experimental designs allow for comparison of the effectiveness of interventions, permitting the team to select the most efficacious intervention, thereby directly addressing the needs of the student(s) (Swanson & Sachse-Lee, 2000).

SINGLE-SUBJECT METHODS AS PART OF RTI

Within the RTI model, single-case experimental design methodology is typically used (1) to compare the relative effectiveness of two or more proposed interventions, (2) to "test drive" an intervention to determine its treatment potential, and (3) to document student performance. Before discussing each of these phases, a review of the basic components of single-subject experimental design is offered.

Basic Components of Single-Subject Experimental Designs

Data Recording Procedures

It all boils down to collecting accurate and meaningful data. We can design and precisely implement a comprehensive student-centered and empirically based intervention, but if we fail to measure accurately the effect of the intervention (i.e., recording the dependent variable) or record irrelevant variables (i.e., the error of misplaced precision), then we are unable to determine with any degree of objectivity whether the student has benefited from the intervention. There are a number of procedures that have been used to measure a wide range of academic, social, and interfering behaviors. Both Steege et al. (2002) and Watson and Steege (2003) offer descriptions and examples of the following types of recording procedures:

- Frequency recording (the number of times a behavior occurs).
- Duration recording (how long a behavior lasts).
- Intensity (the relative magnitude of a behavior).
- Whole-interval recording (percent of intervals in which behavior occurs for an entire interval of time).
- Partial-interval recording (percent of intervals in which behavior occurs for part of the interval).
- Performance-based recording (Likert ratings estimating relative occurrence of behaviors).
- Permanent products recording (tangible outcomes such as number of words spelled correctly).

In order to make certain that the recording methods match the overall objective of the intervention, certain questions should be considered when selecting a behavior recording procedure. Suggested questions are as follows.

- Is the behavior being measured an expected outcome of the intervention?
- Is the behavior recording procedure sensitive enough to measure the expected behavior changes?
- Will the behavior recording procedure capture the magnitude of the behavior? For example, while a frequency recording procedure could be used to measure the occurrences of tantrum behavior, if the duration of tantrums is highly variable (e.g., lasting from 15 seconds to 15 minutes), then a frequency recording procedure may not be a valid measure of the tantrum behavior. (Note: One 15-second tantrum is quite different from one 15-minute tantrum.)
- Are there adequate resources (e.g., time, staff, materials) to collect the data accurately? For example, a 6-second whole-interval recording procedure may be the "gold standard" for measuring on-task behavior. However, there may not be adequate resources to use a whole-interval procedure, and instead a performance-based procedure is selected (see Steege et al., 2001, for an examination of the reliability and accuracy of performance-based recording procedures).

Baseline Phase

It all begins here. The baseline phase provides information about the preintervention level of occurrence of the target behavior (i.e., dependent variable). The baseline data also serve as the basis by which intervention effects are assessed (see Box 5.1). The baseline data serve two critical functions:

1. The baseline describes the current level of occurrence of the student's behaviors and defines the extent of the student's "problems" objectively.
2. The baseline provides a basis for predicting behavior or performance if the intervention is not implemented (Shernoff, Kratochwill, & Stoiber, 2002).

Hayes, Barlow, and Nelson-Grey (1999) suggest that the following five guidelines must be adhered to when establishing baseline levels of behavior or performance:

1. *Length of baseline.* At least three data points are needed to establish a baseline level of behavior or performance.
2. *Stability of baseline.* Stability refers to fluctuations or variability in a student's behavior over time. A baseline is considered to be unstable when variability or trends in behavior eliminate the detection of treatment effects.
3. *Overlap of baseline and intervention data.* When there is considerable overlap between baseline and intervention data (i.e., extreme scores in the baseline are equivalent to or exceed intervention data), the determination that the intervention resulted in the treatment gains is weakened.
4. *Level of the data.* The level of baseline behavior must be serious enough to warrant intervention and be likely to show marked treatment gains.
5. *Trends in the data.* Trends during the baseline period should not be in the desired direction (i.e., an increasing trend when one expects to increase a skill). Figure 5.1 illustrates stable and unstable trends during a baseline-period.

Intervention Phase

Once a stable baseline has been identified, the intervention can begin. This involves implementing the specific procedures related to the intervention. During this phase, the

---

BOX 5.1. How Do I Get Baseline?

If you have already conducted benchmark assessments, you have established a starting point. These data may constitute a baseline, or you may need to conduct additional assessments (i.e., survey-level assessments). Consider the case of a student with reading difficulties. If the student scored "0" on the fall benchmark, additional information about the student's performance is needed. This could include measures of letter-naming fluency, phonemic segmentation, and nonsense-word fluency. Conducting *three separate assessments of each skill* would meet the minimum requirement for establishing baseline levels of performance. Once stability in a baseline has been attained, one is able to implement the intervention.

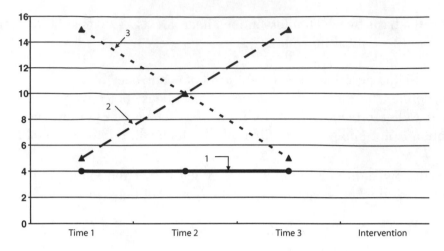

FIGURE 5.1. Baseline descriptions. 1 = Stable baseline. 2 = Stable baseline for behavior that is expected to decrease during intervention; unstable baseline for behavior that is expected to increase during baseline. 3 = Stable baseline for behavior that is expected to increase during intervention; unstable baseline for behavior that is expected to decrease during intervention.

student's behaviors are recorded using the same outcome indicator (dependent variable) that was used during the baseline phase. During this stage it is critical that:

- The intervention be implemented consistently and with precision.
- If an intervention package (i.e., an intervention that has multiple components) has been selected, the entire package be implemented.
- The procedures for recording behavior during baseline be the same procedures used to record the same behaviors during the intervention phase (we want to make sure that we are comparing apples to apples).
- If a change in the intervention is to be implemented, we consider such a change to represent a subsequent phase of the investigation (see Figure 5.2).

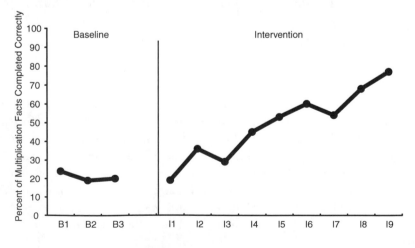

FIGURE 5.2. Case study (AB) design.

Comparing Interventions

Throughout our careers in school psychology practice we have encountered numerous situations in which members of the student assistance team identified two or more competing intervention strategies. Most of you are familiar with this scenario: comprehensive assessments have been conducted, results have been shared, several recommended intervention strategies have been discussed, and now team members are trying to select the one method of choice to use with this student. Or, consider the situation in which an intervention has been recommended as a replacement for an ongoing intervention. The SAT is divided, and members of the team may spend an inordinate amount of time discussing the pros and cons, the merits and disadvantages of each intervention. When teams fail to use a data-based decision-making process, they often become paralyzed with indecision and end up doing nothing. Or they become frustrated and someone makes an "administrative decision" and impulsively selects a specific intervention. Often the selection of intervention is based on insufficient evidence or a subjective factor such as:

- Research to support the intervention ("A study was recently published that demonstrated the effectiveness of the intervention with a group of LD students in a classroom in Kalamazoo, Michigan").
- Anecdotal evidence ("It worked with Johnny—maybe it will work with Jill").
- Familiarity ("I've used this strategy with students for years").
- Intuitive appeal ("This *ought* to work").

When teams are thus divided, single-subject experimental design methodology is a valuable tool for objectively comparing the proposed interventions (see Box 5.2).

Test Driving the Intervention

Let's say you've made the decision to buy a new car. Being a prudent car buyer, you begin the process by first conducting a screening of available makes and models. Based on this initial screening, you narrow your choice to three manufacturers and five different car models. You next begin the assessment phase. You go to dealerships, check out the cars, and request brochures. You go home, study the brochures, comparing the vehicles across a host of dimensions and variables. Next, you turn to the literature (e.g., car magazines, auto reviews online), where you locate several articles in which these cars have been subjected to a variety of performance tests and have been rated for features such as handling, comfort level, dependability, safety, etc. Now comes the really fun part . . . the test drive. This is where you really get a feel for the vehicle . . . where the rubber literally meets the road.

Typically, it's the test drive that determines whether or not this car meets your needs and expectations. How many people walk into a showroom without ever test driving a vehicle and simply say "That's the car for me" and purchase the car on the spot? Not many. However, in school settings, how many times are we asked or do we ask others to try an intervention without conducting a thorough needs assessment, without reviewing

---

BOX 5.2. All the Write Stuff

Steege et al. (2002) described an example in which a student with both cerebral palsy and learning disabilities in the areas of reading comprehension and written language was expected to complete all written assignments using pencil and paper. The school psychologist and special education teacher offered a recommendation that the student be provided with and taught to use a laptop computer to complete written assignments. They hypothesized that by providing her with a laptop computer she would demonstrate an increase in the efficiency, quantity, and quality of written work. Because previous recommendations for a laptop computer for students with disabilities had been denied by the school's administration, they decided to test their hypothesis by using a single-subject experimental design methodology. Using an alternating treatments design (see Figure 5.3), the school psychologist and special educator compared the relative effectiveness of the laptop versus pen/pencil methods in writing performance.

   The results of the assessment clearly demonstrated that, when directly compared with handwriting, the word processor strategy consistently resulted in higher levels of written language performance (Steege et al., 2002). This resulted in the school district's reversing its previous policies and authorizing the purchase of a laptop computer for this student. In this case, the "data did the talking" and allowed the team to make a data-based decision about a course of action that supported the student.

---

the relevant literature, or without taking a test drive? In our experience, all too often this happens—remember facilitated communication (or perhaps you'd just rather forget it)? Within a collaborative problem-solving model, we typically recommend that, following the comprehensive assessment and design of intervention, we conduct a brief "test drive" to "get a feel for the intervention." Specifically, we conduct the test drive of the intervention to answer the following questions:

- Is the intervention effective (i.e., does it result in the expected behavior change or performance)?
- Is the intervention doable, and do we have adequate resources (e.g., time, materials, etc.) to implement the intervention as designed?
- Are staff members implementing the intervention accurately (i.e., observing treatment integrity), and, if not, what types of and how much training are needed?
- Are the data recording procedures valid (i.e., matched to the dimensions of the behavior and recording meaningful behavior change)?
- Are staff members able to collect the data accurately?
- Are there aspects of the interventions that need to be modified?

A clear advantage of taking a "test drive" approach is that, if the answer to any of the preceding questions is "maybe" or "no," then the necessary modifications to increase the effectiveness of the intervention, its implementation, and the recording of data can be made before too much time passes and the student's school success is at risk.

Documenting Student Performance over Time

Having completed a successful test drive, we are now ready to implement the intervention. Essentially this involves implementing the intervention and continuing to record and analyze the student's response to the intervention over time. Ongoing data collection serves three important purposes. First, continued recording of behavioral outcomes allows for objective documentation of student progress on specific goals and objectives. Second, analysis of data enables team members to make data-based decisions about whether or not to modify the intervention. Third, continued measurement allows for objective determination of the degree of effectiveness of the intervention.

CASE EXAMPLES

The following case examples illustrate the application of single-subject experimental design methods within a problem-solving model of school-based practice.

Case Study

In the following case study, the design (two phases: baseline followed by intervention) was used to document the effects of the intervention during the "test drive" phase of a math intervention. Noreen is a fourth-grade student who has not yet learned her multiplication facts. Her teacher is concerned about this and decided to conduct an individualized session with Noreen to work on this material. In order to determine Noreen's baseline multiplication fact skills, her teacher gave her multiplication fact probes with 25 problems on each page (see Table 5.1 for operational definitions of the math intervention variables). Noreen was given 2 minutes to complete each page, and the percentage of correct answers was recorded on a graph. Data from the baseline and intervention phases of this case study are shown in Figure 5.2. During the baseline phase, Noreen got between 20 and 25% of the problems correct. After implementation of the individualized sessions with her teacher, Noreen's multiplication fact accuracy increased to 80%.

Interpretation

This intervention was determined to be successful, because the data revealed that it resulted in the desired outcome of improving Noreen's multiplication fact skills.

TABLE 5.1. Operational Definitions of Noreen's Math Intervention Variables

Target behavior(s)	Recording procedure(s)	Dependent variable
Accurate completion of randomly selected multiplication facts in vertical number format	Student completes multiplication problems while being timed for 2 minutes	Percent of multiplication facts completed correctly

The drawback to the case study single-subject design is that it does not include review of data collected over a long period of time or when the target skill is used in another setting. In Noreen's case, the obtained data provided a good "test drive" in that they documented that the sessions with her teacher resulted in improved skills. Still, Noreen's newly gained multiplication skills are of limited value if they are only used during individual sessions with her teacher. To learn whether these skills generalize, at least one additional intervention phase would be needed to evaluate Noreen's accuracy in multiplying numbers in another setting, such as while doing independent work in class or on a test. The following examples show how application of multiple single-subject design phases produces better and more educationally relevant data.

Multiple-Baseline across Behaviors Design with Generalization

In this example, Teddy is a third-grade student who has struggled on his weekly spelling tests. Baseline data about Teddy's spelling accuracy revealed a consistent 25% spelling accuracy rate on three tests (see Figure 5.3). Teddy's teacher implemented a new spelling intervention designed to improve his spelling accuracy. Table 5.2 includes operational definitions of spelling intervention variables. This intervention involved direct instruction on the sounds in words to help Teddy learn the correct spelling of specific words. In order to learn whether Teddy generalized the spelling skills to other words not specifically taught, his teacher evaluated his progress with two sets of words: (1) words taught

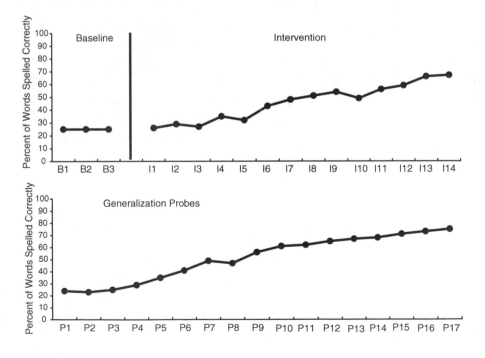

FIGURE 5.3. Multiple-baseline across behaviors design with generalization.

TABLE 5.2. Operational Definitions of Spelling Intervention Variables

Target behavior(s)	Recording procedure(s)	Dependent variable
Accurate spelling of words on weekly spelling tests	Student writes spelling words dictated by teacher	Percent of words spelled correctly

and (2) words not taught. Teddy's progress in spelling was monitored by having him take a weekly spelling test that included an equal number of both sets of words. In order to evaluate the efficacy of the program on Teddy's spelling of both word sets, his accuracy rate on each set of words was graphed separately. As shown in Figure 5.3, Teddy's spelling accuracy improved, and he was able to spell about 65% of both word sets correctly at the end of 13 weeks of instruction.

Interpretation

These data support the hypothesis that direct instruction of letter–sound correspondence resulted in increases in spelling accuracy on word set 1. Skills acquired during intervention with word set 1 generalized to word set 2. Thus, direct instruction with additional word samples was not indicated.

Multiple-Baseline across Behaviors Design without Generalization

The next example is very similar to the preceding one (Teddy). It shows how the use of a multiple-baseline across behaviors design can be used to assess the generalizability of skills from two word sets, but with staggered implementation of intervention and with two maintenance probes at a later date. In this case, Max, one of Teddy's classmates, began the same spelling intervention, but slightly different recording procedures were used. In Max's case, he did not appear to generalize the correct spelling of the words not taught. This is seen in Figure 5.4, where the top portion of the graph depicts performance on taught words and the bottom portion depicts performance on words not taught. Because Max continued to spell the untaught words with only about 20% accuracy, 2 weeks after the spelling intervention began his teacher started teaching him both sets or words using the same explicit procedures. Within 2 weeks of the explicit spelling instruction Max's spelling performance improved to about 40%. After 10 sessions he spelled all the words with about 80% accuracy.

Due to Max's lack of generalization of the untaught words at the beginning of the intervention, his teacher decided to do some follow-up skill maintenance probes with him. A number of weeks after the intervention ended, she gave Max two spelling tests, 1 week apart. Max correctly spelled about 80% of the words on the maintenance phase spelling tests, indicating that he maintained the spelling skills learned during the intervention.

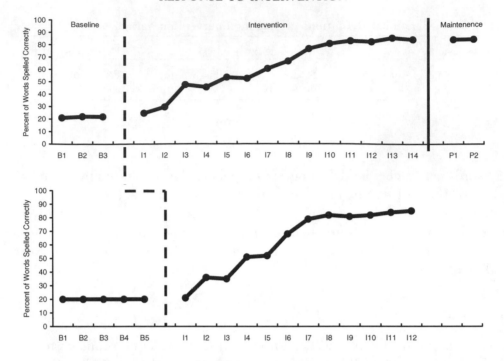

FIGURE 5.4. Multiple-baseline across behaviors design without generalization.

Interpretation

These data support the hypothesis that direct and systematic instruction of spelling words from word set 1 resulted in increases in accurate spelling of the words on weekly tests. Generalization of acquired skills to word list 2 did not occur. Implementation of the intervention with word set 2 resulted in the acquisition of the relevant knowledge. Thus, when—and only when—the intervention was implemented did improvements in student behavior occur.

Alternating Interventions

In the next example an alternating interventions design was used to compare the relative effectiveness of two different interventions for Megan, a fifth-grade student. Megan's accuracy on spelling tests at the beginning of the school year was very poor. She got less than 20% of words correct over 3 weeks. Her teacher was very worried because spelling is one of the subtests on the state's fifth-grade achievement test. Those students who fail two or more sections of the test must repeat the fifth grade. Megan's teacher discussed her concern about Megan's spelling with the special education consultant. The consultant suggested the use of a phonics-based spelling program. Megan's teacher was all set to use this method when she overheard another teacher in the faculty room saying that the copy–cover–say spelling instruction method was best. The teacher asked her colleague why she felt the copy–cover–say method was best and was told it had worked "for years and years." Megan's teacher felt uncertain which spelling instruction method was best, so she decided to try them both and see how Megan responded to the two interventions.

Megan's teacher used a counterbalanced implementation of the two interventions so that the effects of the two different instructional methods could be compared. First, 100 phonetically regular words were split into two sets of 50 words each. Each set of 50 words was matched to one of two spelling instruction methods: (1) systematic phonics and (2) copy–cover–say. In the systematic phonics spelling instruction the teacher taught the students to spell the phonetically regular words by having them match the sounds in the words to the letters or letter combinations (orthographic units) that match the sounds. For example, students learned to spell the word *hat* by identifying each of the sounds in the word—/h/a/t/—and writing each letter corresponding to the sounds. The copy–cover–say spelling instruction method involved giving the students 10 new phonetically regular words each week and having them copy each word five times. Once they had written each word five times, they folded their papers in half to cover the words and they said the spellings aloud. The two lesson types were counterbalanced by alternating each type every other school day.

Student progress in each of these methods was monitored by giving one spelling test at the end of each week that consisted of 20 spelling words, with half the words from the phonics lessons and the other half from the copy–cover–say method. Results for one of the students, Megan, are shown in Figure 5.5. The percentage of words that Megan spelled correctly is shown along the Y axis. The solid line on the graph shows the percentage of phonics lesson words she spelled correctly; the dashed line shows the number of copy–cover–say words she spelled correctly. The graph indicates that Megan learned to spell words from the phonics lessons with about 80% accuracy, but spelled the copy–cover–say words with only about 20% accuracy.

Interpretation

These data support the hypothesis that intervention 1 (i.e., systematic phonics-based spelling) was more effective in increasing Megan's rate of correctly spelled words than intervention 2 (i.e., copy–cover–say).

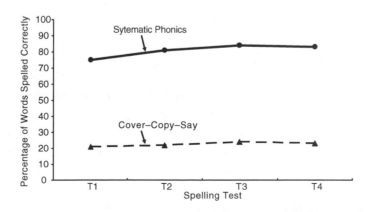

FIGURE 5.5. Alternating interventions.

Comparing Performance across Multiple Dependent Variables

The last case study example was used to document the effectiveness of reading fluency instruction for increasing performance on three separate dependent variables (e.g., sight word, fluency, and comprehension). This method was used to learn whether a specific reading fluency intervention would lead to improvements in sight word reading and comprehension as well as increased reading fluency. The design was employed with Gavin, a seventh-grade student with reading difficulties. Gavin began his seventh-grade year by telling his language arts teacher that he "hates reading." The teacher asked Gavin why he hated to read, and Gavin replied, "It takes too long. Asking someone is faster." Gavin's teacher decided it would be good to learn more about Gavin's reading skills, so he had Gavin complete three curriculum-based measurement (CBM) silent-reading fluency (SRF) passages. CBM–SRF passages are reading level-controlled texts from which every seventh word has been replaced with a line. Under the line are three words from which the reader selects while reading. Only one of the three word choices is the correct word. Students are timed while they read the passages; in this case, Gavin's teacher gave the passages to all of the students in Gavin class, and they had 3 minutes to complete each passage.

Gavin obtained scores of 1, 1, and 0 on the three passages. The average score for the class was 15 correct selections on each passage. Due to Gavin's very low score as compared to other students, his teacher decided to measure his reading with two other assessments. First, she had Gavin read three CBM oral reading fluency (ORF) passages. On these passages Gavin read aloud for 1 minute while his teacher recorded his errors on her own copy of the passage. Gavin obtained scores of 21 on all three ORF passages. The national fall ORF benchmark for seventh grade students was 110 words in 1 minute. The teacher then had Gavin read isolated sight words on 3″ × 5″ cards. The words were selected from a list of the 500 most common words in English literature. From a bank of 20 words, Gavin was able to read 18 correctly. Based on the three reading data sets collected, Gavin's teacher concluded that he could read (decode) most words but that he read only very slowly. The lack of fluency in Gavin's reading appeared to interfere with his reading comprehension.

Gavin's teacher decided to try a reading fluency intervention to improve his reading skills. The intervention involved having Gavin practice reading both sight words and connected text every day for 20 minutes. Definitions for each activity in the interventions are found in Table 5.3. First he took a set of 20 sight words and read them aloud to the teacher. She recorded his accuracy. Next, Gavin read a controlled-level text silently to himself five times. Finally, he wrote a summary of the short story to show what he learned from it. At the end of each week Gavin completed three assessments of his reading improvement. First he read a random selection of 20 of the 500 common sight words while his teacher recorded his accuracy. Next, he completed a CBM–ORF passage and recorded his progress. Finally, Gavin completed a CBM–SRF passage and recorded the number of correct word choices on a graph. These data are summarized in Figure 5.6. The data show that Gavin improved his sight-word reading a small amount, going from

TABLE 5.3. Operational Definitions of Reading Intervention Variables

Target behavior(s)	Recording procedure(s)	Dependent variable
Sight word reading	Teacher holds up 3″ × 5″ cards with taught words on them; student reads words and teacher records if correct or incorrect.	Number of correctly read isolated sight words
Reading fluency	Student orally reads a reading-level controlled short story for 1 minute; teacher records all misread words while the student reads.	Number of words read correctly in 1 minute
Reading comprehension	Student silently reads a reading-level-controlled short story for 3 minutes; the story has been adapted so that every seventh word is replaced with a blank line under which are three words. While reading the student circles one of the three words to fill in the blanks in the story.	Number of correct word selections made in 3 minutes

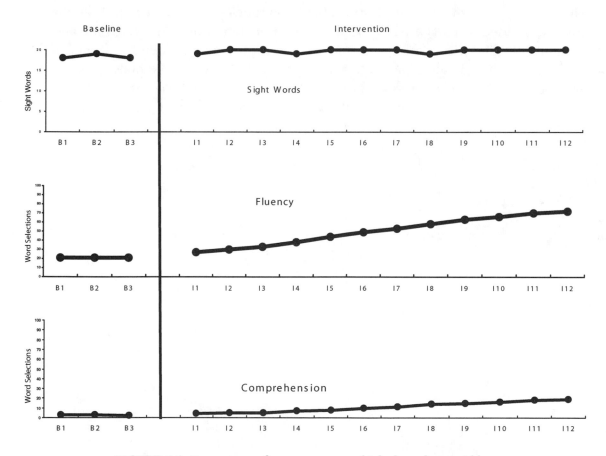

FIGURE 5.6. Comparing performance across multiple dependent variables.

90–95% accuracy (i.e., 18–19 correct answers out of 20) to 100% (20 of 20) accuracy. His ORF score went from 21 words read correctly during baseline to 77 words at the end of 12 weeks. Gavin's SRF score improved from 1 correct word selection to 18 correct selections.

Interpretation

These data support the hypothesis that the reading fluency (speed) intervention was effective in increasing all three reading skills. In this example, daily practice in reading sight words as well as short stories resulted in not only an increase in sight-word accuracy but also concomitant increases in reading fluency and comprehension.

SUMMARY

This chapter has provided information about how single-subject research design methods can be used as part of RTI procedures to promote positive academic outcomes for students. Starting with a basic case study design to "test drive" an intervention and following up with generalization and maintenance, or instructional methods comparisons, was shown to lead to better skills for students across several school learning areas. Next we will describe how RTI methods fit into comprehensive student support systems.

6

Single-Subject Research and RTI

A Natural Collaboration

INTEGRATING EMPIRICALLY BASED INSTRUCTION AND DATA

The last two chapters have provided information about the importance of scientifically based instruction methods and single-subject data collection methods. This chapter will include a discussion of how empirically validated practices can be combined with single-subject research methods to yield effective response to intervention practices. The instructional and data collection methods we will cover reflect the emerging legal standards found in No Child Left Behind Act and the Individuals with Disabilities Education Improvement Act. As noted in Chapters 2 and 3, these education policies seek to integrate general and special education practices such that effective instruction is provided to *all* students from the very beginning of their educational careers. This chapter will begin with a discussion of the features of effective instruction, followed by review of and synthesis with the features of effective data collection and analysis procedures. As explained in Figure 1.1 in Chapter 1, together these are the cornerstones of RTI.

KEY FEATURES OF EFFECTIVE INSTRUCTION

Chapter 4 of this volume provided a definition as well as a discussion of empirically based instruction. When connecting empirically based instruction to RTI practices, empirically based instruction is the essence of *effective* instruction. In order for any instructional practice, program, or intervention to be considered effective, it must be empirically based. Thus effective instruction includes only those practices that have been validated in numerous research studies. In order to make sense of the voluminous information about effective instructional practices, we have synthesized the findings into a core set of *effective* instructional features and practices. Following from work by Kame'enui and Carnine (1998), our list will focus on the "big ideas" about effective instruction. Table 6.1 includes a summary of the key features of effective instructional practices. There are 5 main features and 11 practices that define empirically based *effective* instruction. The five features are (1) content, (2) delivery, (3) pace, (4) responses, and (5) assessment. The practices related to the features are the teaching methods associated with positive educational outcomes for learners.

Content

The first key feature seen in effective instruction is appropriate content. This refers to the substance of what is to be learned. For example, in a language arts class it could be the eight parts of speech or the difference between active and passive sentence construction. There are two main teaching practices that are associated with effective and empirically based content selection. The first of these is matching the content to the larger curriculum or program of study. A number of studies have shown that when teaching content matches with and complements an overall program of study, specific lessons and activities are more effective (Carnine, 1981, 1989; Carnine & Jitendra, 1997). Specifically, when a lesson is matched to the larger set of knowledge and skills that students are expected to learn or need to know in order to progress in the curriculum and school program, the individual learning content is more likely to be mastered by students (Gibb & Wilder, 2002).

TABLE 6.1. Scientifically Based Instructional Components and Practices

Component	Practices
Content	1. Matched to that which students are expected to learn or need to know in order to progress in the curriculum and school program. 2. Fits in between the knowledge and/or skills that students have previously learned or will learn in subsequent instruction.
Delivery	1. Explicit description of knowledge and/or skills to be learned is given by the teacher. 2. Students are given many and frequent opportunities to rehearse the new knowledge and/or skills. 3. All students are actively engaged with the knowledge and/or skills to be learned throughout the lesson.
Pace	1. Intensive "massed" practice of new material is provided during the early stages of learning. 2. Judicious review of previously learned knowledge and skills is incorporated at regular intervals.
Responses	1. Correct student responses are reinforced by the teacher with verbal praise or specific reinforcers. 2. Incorrect student responses are addressed immediately during the lesson and followed with student rehearsal of the correct response.
Assessment	1. Students are assessed continuously during the lesson; daily student performance data are recorded. 2. Summative data about student progress is reviewed at least weekly to determine whether instructional changes are needed.

A second important practice related to subject matter content is sequencing individual lessons in an order that allows new information to build on prior learning (Bransford, Brown, & Cocking, 2000; Cognition and Technology Group at Vanderbilt, 1997). Studies of "experts" in a number of different fields have shown that when instruction follows an "order of operations" it is easier to master the learning. In the case of school-age students, teachers need to have some idea of what students have learned previously as well as what will be taught in subsequent grades. For example, in the case of elementary mathematics instruction, it is important that teachers know that addition is usually the focus of first grade and subtraction the focus of second grade. When teachers work within the context of an identified skill sequence, they are better able to provide instruction that fits in between the knowledge and/or skills that students have previously learned and what they will learn in subsequent instruction (Bransford, 1979).

Delivery

The second major feature of effective instruction is the delivery method. This refers to method(s) that teachers use to present information and solicit student learning. Delivery methods include lectures, discussions, inquiry activities, and assigned readings. There are three teaching delivery practices most associated with positive outcomes for students (Williams & Carnine, 1981). First, direct and explicit description of the knowledge and/or skills to be learned is given by the teacher to the students. Examples of direct and explicit instruction include telling students the general topic to be covered as well as the precise details, rules, and operating procedures necessary to carry out the learning correctly (Engelmann, 1999; Carnine, Kame'enui, & Maggs, 1982; Gersten & Carnine, 1986; Stein, Carnine, & Dixon, 1989). The second delivery method most associated with positive learning outcomes is giving students many and frequent opportunities to rehearse the new knowledge and/or skills (see Box 6.1). For example, when students need to learn their multiplication facts, learners of all ability levels are more likely to do this if they are provided with many opportunities to rehearse (i.e., practice, practice, practice) each fact many times (Carnine, 1997b). The third important delivery practice is to provide students with continuous exposure to the content. This means that the learning materials need to be physically present and accessible to the students while they engage in learning activities. In the case of learning multiplication facts, each student needs to have his or her own set of multiplication fact cards to review, practice, review. High levels of learner engagement with content have consistently been associated with positive learning outcomes for all students (Carnine, 1989).

Pace

The third major feature of effective instruction is pace (see Box 6.2). High-quality lessons that promote student learning have a pace that follows the "Goldilocks" principle: it is neither too fast nor too slow, but it is "just right." The right pace for a lesson is related to the content to be taught and the place in the curriculum where the material falls. Knowledge and skills in the early part of a program of study will need to be covered more

BOX 6.1. Practice, Practice, Practice

Anyone who has ever tried to learn a new skill knows the importance of practice. This is true whether the skill is playing the piano or throwing a baseball. Those who put time into practicing achieve better results and more "perfect" performance than those who do not. Even the top musicians and athletes practice many hours every day to improve their skills. When a famous violin player wants to learn a new piece of music, he or she must start by looking at the individual notes, play them in the correct order, and then practice the piece countless time to get it right. If a competitive diver wants to learn a new dive, he must practice each part the put the moves together into one smooth action that makes it look easy. But it's not. Perfect, or near perfect, performance comes from practice, practice, practice.

The same is true of academic skills such as reading, writing, and mathematics. Those who learn the subcomponents, put them together, and then practice by using the skills regularly are better readers, writers, and math users than those who look briefly at a word or number but never practice using it. The importance of practice in everyday classroom instruction has been shown in many research studies (Carnine, 1989) and needs to be integrated into all levels of RTI activities in order for students to make the progress we expect and desire.

BOX 6.2. Slow Learner or Fast Teacher?

Some students who are referred for special education—and even some who receive such instruction—are able to be successful in school if the pace of instruction is matched to how quickly they can handle the material. For example, many students who have been identified as having a learning disability are allowed extra time to complete tasks, including exams. Another way of looking at the needs of such students would be to ask: "is the teaching too fast?" This question radically changes the way we look at the difficulties students have in schools. Instead of assuming that a student is doing poorly because the student has limitations—is a slow learner—with a comprehensive assessment of student and instructional variables we may find a mismatch between the "slow" learner and the "fast" teacher.

We've previously discussed the importance of monitoring the pace of instruction—instruction that is too fast may result in errors and compromised acquisition of skills. This issue has important implications for RTI practices, because one of the ways to test a hypothesis about a student's school performance is to assess and change environmental variables. The teacher is an environmental variable that can be adjusted. In fact, when teachers are empowered to create changes in instructional materials and methods, students' knowledge and skills are maximized. Given that there is ample evidence showing that the pace of instruction influences learner outcomes, teachers need to be given the resources and autonomy to adjust the rate of classroom activities as part of the intervention process. RTI methods provide the team with data-based recommendations for making student-centered changes that result in meaningful and enduring outcomes.

slowly, but information contained in later sections of the program can be taught at a faster pace (Bransford et al., 2000; Carnine & Granzin, 2001). Two instructional practices that inform and shape the pace are massed practice and judicious review (Kame'enui & Carnine, 1998). Massed practice refers to a lesson time when all of the activities relate to one area of learning. These lessons have a clear and single focus and revolve around students learning something specific. An example of massed practice is having students learn, review, and repeat the names of the presidents of the United States until they can say them with a high degree of accuracy. The other important instructional pacing practice is judicious review. This refers to having students recall to mind and use previously learned information on a regular interval so that it remains in their knowledge or skill sets over a long period of time. An example of judicious review would be to include study and recall of certain presidents on a regular basis so that students continuously know this information.

Responses

The fourth key feature of effective instruction relates to student–teacher interactions during lessons. Specifically, it is the responses that the students and teachers make to each other that characterize effective instructional responses. Teachers need to provide reinforcement of correct student responses so that students know when they are correct. Providing validation and reinforcement to students as they learn increases the likelihood that students will use those same responses again in the future. Nonetheless, when students give incorrect answers or performances, teachers need to provide immediate correction procedures. This step is important because it prevents students from learning incorrect information. Teachers need to address student incorrect responses immediately during the lesson and follow them with student rehearsal of the correct response. Importantly, regardless of the student's answer, teachers need to provide immediate feedback to the student in order to maximize accurate learning.

Assessment

The last key feature of effective instruction is assessment. There are two assessment activities that are critical for effective instruction. These can be summarized as formative and summative evaluation procedures, but they are more specific than general methods. Effective instruction includes formative assessments as part of the instructional design. Formative assessments are those that happen at regular intervals along the way toward a specific learning goal. These assessments allow both the student and the teacher to determine whether the student is making progress toward the instructional goals. Specifically, in effective formative assessment practices students are assessed continuously during the lesson, and daily student performance data are recorded to track student progress. This supports effective instruction because, if the data show that a student is not making progress, the teacher can reteach certain lessons before moving on to more difficult material. Importantly, if a student needs more intensive or lengthy instruction on a regular basis, the obtained formative data can be used to help determine whether a student needs specialized instructional support. If, alternatively, all or most of the students in a class do poorly on an assessment, it may reflect that the instruction was not effective and other teaching methods are needed.

The final effective teaching practice is the use of summative assessment. Although formative data are a cornerstone of effective instruction, summative data are also important because they allow the student and teacher to reflect on whether a student achieved goals set in the overall instructional program. For example, just as formative data about medical students' knowledge of anatomy, physiology, and chemistry are important indicators of their mastery of key health-related details, summative information about how well they can synthesize discrete facts well enough to treat live patients is also essential. School-age children benefit from summative assessment as well because it offers a way of determining how well they have learned the core skills necessary to be productive citizens. When formative and summative assessment data are combined, they offer comprehensive and powerful indicators of students' learning progress. They are essential for effective instruction because they indicate whether the other instructional practices utilized by teachers are achieving the desired goals related to student success.

KEY FEATURES OF DATA COLLECTION AND ANALYSIS

As outlined in Chapter 1, data-based decision making is a linchpin of RTI. In order for the data used for RTI decisions to be useful it needs to be reliable and valid. As pointed out in Chapter 5, there are a number of reliable and valid ways to use data to document the efficacy of specific instructional procedures. Whether one uses group-based or single-subject research designs to learn about the effectiveness of an instructional program, there are common features of effective data collection and analysis that must be used so that the obtained data will be worthwhile (see Table 6.2). There are four key features of effective data collection and analysis that can enhance the likelihood that RTI procedures will yield positive outcomes for most students. These are (1) defining the target skill or behavior, (2) specifying the setting(s) where data will be collected, (3) using an accurate data recording format, and (4) conducting careful data analysis and interpretation.

Target Skill or Behavior

The first step in collecting accurate data for RTI decision making is to define the target skill or behavior that needs to be evaluated. By having a clear and precise definition of the skill or behavior that is to be taught, the data collected about that behavior are more likely to be accurate and useful (Steege et al., 2002; Watson & Steege, 2003). Importantly, the desired skill or behavior needs to be operationally defined in clear language that includes topography, frequency, duration, and intensity. Topography refers to the shape, or "look," of the behavior. Frequency refers to how often the behavior happens. In some cases the duration of the behavior is a critical part of the definition, because it is only

TABLE 6.2. Data Collection and Analysis Components and Practices

Components	Practices
Target skill or behavior	1. The desired skill or behavior is operationally defined in clear language that includes topography, frequency, duration, and intensity. 2. Code(s) for the specific skill(s) or behavior(s) are developed to be used during data collection.
Setting(s)	1. The location(s) where the skills or behaviors will be observed and recorded are described. 2. If more than one setting is identified, codes for the specific settings are developed.

Data recording format	1. Data recording procedures and materials are developed that specify:
	  a. Who will collect data.
	  b. Where data will be recorded.
	  c. When data will be recorded.
	  d. How data will be recorded.
	2. If needed, the materials necessary for recording data are collected and stored in an accessible location.

Analysis and interpretation	1. Once a specified amount of data are collected, the obtained information is reviewed to determine whether the intervention method produced the desired outcomes. 2. Data are used to revise, increase, decrease, or discontinue the intervention.

while the behavior is happening that interference with the student's learning is a concern. Finally, the intensity of the behavior refers to the extent to which the behavior is problematic and extreme. For example, certain self-injurious behaviors are very "intense" because they are life-threatening. These behaviors (e.g., head banging) need to be addressed more quickly than others because they are more intense and serious (Watson & Steege, 2003).

A second practice related to the target skill or behavior is to create code(s) by which the behavior(s) can be identified during data collection so that data recording can be fast and accurate. For example, in the case of on-task classroom behavior, the operational definition could be:

> Student is looking at the stimulus materials related to the assigned task and performing visual, motor, or verbal tasks to accompany the assignment.

The codes to accompany this definition would need to be dichotomous and document that the student was either on-task, as defined above, or off-task. In other words, the student can be coded as either on-task or off-task, but not both at the same time. Since the definition includes visual, verbal, or motor behaviors to accompany the assigned task, it could be helpful to include in the codes identifiers for the target behavior (OT), as well as codes for when the student is off-task visually (OVi), off-task verbally (OVe), and off-task motorically (OM). Together, these codes provide a way to document what the student does during each of the intervals when the student was observed. Importantly, all those who will be observing the target behavior(s) need to practice using them in training sessions so that everyone applies them in consistent ways.

Setting(s)

In addition to detailing descriptions of the behaviors and codes to be used with them, it is important to determine in advance the settings where the observations will be conducted. Specifically, the environmental conditions and antecedents related to the target behaviors(s) need to be described. This is important because the environment may contribute to the obtained data in important ways. If the same or different observers collect observations but do not note or explain the setting(s) in which the data were collected, the nature of the obtained information may vary in important ways. Importantly, in the case of RTI, data should be collected in specified settings so that the effects and interactions between and among the variables can be investigated. If data need to be collected in more than one setting, then codes for each setting need to be developed as well.

Data Recording Procedures

A third and critical feature of effective data collection and analysis is to develop data recording procedures and materials that specify who will collect data, where data will be recorded, when data will be recorded, and how data will be recorded. A number of already made data recording forms are available, so it may not be necessary for individual teachers and others to create new forms for each situation. A number of forms are found in Watson and Steege (2003) and Shapiro (2004). Additional tools for creating materials may be found at www.interventioncentral.org (Syracuse Public Schools, 2004). An associated practice that is important for promoting effective data collection materials is to collect and organize them in locations where data collectors can access them quickly when needed.

Analysis and Interpretation

The final feature of data-based decision making is data analysis and interpretation. There are two practices that define this stage. First, once a specified amount of data are collected, the obtained information is reviewed to determine whether the intervention method produced the desired outcomes. This involves comparing an individual student's obtained scores with those that were set as goals for that student. There are two major aspects of the data that should be considered: level and slope. Level refers to the score value obtained by the student on a given measure. For example, a student's raw score on a math test would provide an indicator of the student's math level. A level score can be used to identify how an individual student's math performance compares to other students. The second way to review student data is to look at slope. Slope is the rate of progress that a student is making. For example, the number of new words that a student can read correctly each week reflects the student's rate of progress. Slope data reveal how quickly a student is moving toward a goal; slope data can be used to predict whether a student will meet a specific goal in a given period of time.

Both level and slope data are important. If only level data are used, a student may be seen to make progress, but it cannot be determined if the progress will be adequate to meet learning goals. Similarly, if only slope data are used, a student may be observed to make good progress, but the relative standing of that student's skill as compared to his or her peers will not be known. Thus, the first step in data analysis is to review the level and slope data to identify a student's current standing and progress. The first practice leads directly to the second when data are used to revise, increase, decrease, or discontinue the intervention. Decisions about how to proceed with a student's instructional program are made on the basis of whether the student's level and slope data indicate progress toward a specific goal. One of the best ways of interpreting student data is to use the single-subject methods described in Chapter 5.

SUMMARY

When evidence-based instruction is used along with regular data collection, RTI methods are the natural result. While it is possible to collect data from non-evidence-based instruction, such practices are not as likely to enhance the likelihood that all students will make effectual educational progress. However, when evidence-based practices are used, the data collected as part of instruction allow teachers to shape and reshape instruction to optimize outcomes for all students. In order to illustrate how RTI promotes positive outcomes for students, the next chapter will feature a step-by-step discussion of RTI procedures as well as case examples using RTI for academic and behavior problems.

7

Using RTI Procedures for Assessment of Academic Difficulties

USING RTI TO MEET STUDENTS' NEEDS

As outlined in Chapter 3, RTI methods can be used both as general policies to address the needs of all students as well as in specific ways to implement interventions for individual students. This chapter presents examples of what RTI "looks like" when used on a districtwide basis, including the phases focusing on individual students. To assist in describing the steps necessary to implement RTI procedures, we developed a 10-item RTI implementation checklist (see Form 7.1 at the end of the chapter). This checklist provides an overview of the major steps needed to implement RTI. Some of these steps include a number of other activities, so we have also included worksheets for specific RTI steps to assist with planning and implementation of each part of the process (see Forms 7.2–7.11 at the end of the chapter). Interspersed with descriptions of the 10 RTI steps we present case examples of specific steps.

Step 1: Implement Evidence-Based General Education Instructional Methods

The first step in using RTI procedures is to select and implement evidence-based general education practices. This means that all teachers at every grade level need to have scientifically based instructional materials that they use systematically with all students. The *Reading First* materials refer to the general education reading curriculum as a "core" program. Importantly, all "core" materials need to be validated and shown to be evidence-based before they are adopted by a school district. Research has shown that high-quality instructional materials can make a difference in student learning (Carnine & Carnine, 2004). Many teachers, as well as the general public, may believe that all published educational materials have been verified in scientific research. Sadly, this is not true. There is no "Surgeon General's warning" or Food and Drug Administration approval process for teaching materials (Stein, Stuen, Carnine, & Long, 2001). While the new standards about evidence-based instruction found in Reading First and NCLB may lead to such a system, at the present time school personnel have the responsibility for choosing teaching materials that will yield optimal student outcomes. This responsibility means that teachers, principals, and curriculum coordinators need to know how to identify and verify evidence-based materials from the vast array of educational products on the market.

Selecting Effective Teaching Tools

There are a number of activities that can help educators choose high-quality evidence-based instructional tools. These activities fall into three categories: (1) professional development, (2) field research, and (3) expert consultation. Professional development activities include both preservice and in-service learning. At the preservice level, all teaching, administrator, and specialist students need to take at least one class in effective teaching practices (e.g., educational psychology) and at least one class in research methods. A grounding in educational psychology provides educators with a broad knowledge of what specific instructional methods are most effective for the largest number of students. Knowledge of research methods provides educators with the skills to evaluate the strength of the evidence for any given teaching tool. Courses in research methods should include basic statistics, research designs, reliability, validity, and the importance of using research methods matched to the characteristics and features of the target population for which the product has been developed (Carnine & Gersten, 2000).

Once educators have knowledge and skills in effective teaching methods and research principles, they can go on to engage in their own field research activities. Such research includes learning about and critically evaluating teaching materials (e.g., "core" curricula) that they are considering for adoption (U.S. Department of Education, 2004). Field research includes a number of stages, such as locating possible curricula in publishers' catalogs and websites, reviewing the research results from applications of the curriculum, visiting schools where the curriculum is being used, and connecting the proposed curriculum to local instructional goals (Stein et al., 2001). In many cases, educators may be doing some or all of these "research" activities but may not be doing them systematically across the district or for every subject area. To promote more systematic use of curriculum field research, Form 7.2 (at the end of the chapter) provides a reproducible worksheet that can be used to accompany curriculum research. A completed version of the worksheet is found in Figure 7.1. In this example, three specific general education primary grade reading curricula were reviewed. The data revealed that two of the three were evaluated scientifically. Both Open Court and Read Well have data indicating they are effective in teaching reading. In order for a school district to decide which one to select, personnel would need to select which curriculum best matches the local instructional goals.

After a specific general education curriculum has been chosen, it needs to be implemented in all classrooms with a high degree of consistency (Telzrow, McNamara, & Hollinger, 2000). Just as effective RTI practices need to be implemented correctly, instructional materials need to be used in classrooms in ways that yield consistent results

Program	Publisher (Date)	Research Evidence	Connections to Local Goals	Observations
Open Court	SRA (2005)	Focrman, B., Francis, D., Fletcher, J., Schatschneider, C., & Mehta, P. (1998). The role of instruction in learning to read: Preventing reading failure in at-risk children. *Journal of Educational Psychology, 90,* 37–55. This study of 285 first- and second-grade students compared three types of classroom reading programs: (1) direct instruction in sound-spelling correspondences (Open Court Reading); (2) less direct instruction in sound-spelling correspondences; and (3) implicit instructions in the alphabetic code as part of reading connected text. Results showed better outcomes for children in the Open Court group.	Our local goals include direct, systematic teaching of phonics in general education classrooms	We observed an Open Court lesson at Wedgewood Elementary, and the students were highly engaged and learning.
Read Well	Sopris West (2002)	Jitendra, A. K., Edwards, L. L., Starosta, K., Sacks, G., Jacobson, L. A., & Choutka, C. M. (2004). *Journal of Learning Disabilities, 37,* 421–440. Differences in student characteristics and in the amount of Read Well instruction received (2 to 7 weeks) seemed to account for differences in performance. Overall, the findings from Year 1 and 2 studies indicate the benefits of Read Well's instructional intensity and duration for children who struggle with emerging reading skills.	Read Well puts a heavy focus on repeated practice of phonics skills, an area of emphasis in our local goals.	Observation of students in a Read Well classroom showed that each had his/her own materials and were practicing independently.
Houghton Mifflin Reading	Houghton Mifflin (2005)	No research found.	This new program is advertised as integrating phonics with graded literature-based texts.	Observation of students in a grade 1 classroom showed that students were eager to use the software but not as engaged with their workbooks.

FIGURE 7.1. Example of a completed Instructional Materials Review Worksheet.

across learners. In an ideal world, all curricula would not only be evidence-based but also come with implementation checklists. Such checklists, like the one provided in this chapter for RTI, are stepwise lists of all the steps necessary to use a set of materials and methods with a high degree of accuracy and consistency. The process of checking the implementation of a procedure is known as treatment fidelity and has been shown to have a significant role in achieving the desired outcomes (Sanetti & Kratochwill, 2005). If an implementation checklist is not provided for a curriculum, one can be created by analyzing the essential elements needed to implement the instruction so that students learn the intended material. A blank intervention integrity checklist is found in Form 7.3 at the end of the chapter. This checklist can be used by both classroom teachers for self-evaluation of intervention integrity or by observers who record whether all steps in completing a lesson are done correctly. In cases when subsets of a curriculum are selected for use to teach specific learning, it is important to create an implementation checklist so that all teachers use the same materials and steps.

An example of a completed intervention integrity checklist is found in Figure 7.2. In this example Ms. Jones completed a self-evaluation of her correct implementation of a specific reading lesson when she introduced the letter *B*. She wrote in the date, time, and topic of the lesson and then checked "yes" or "no" to indicate whether she had completed each step. For those steps which she did not complete, Ms. Jones wrote a note indicating what happened that prevented the correct implementation of those steps. Checklists such as this one can be used to monitor and review the extent of consistency and accuracy of implementation of RTI interventions at Tiers 1 and 2. Intervention integrity checklists provide a way to ensure that all teachers who are using a specific curriculum use it in the same way so that students have the benefit of highly consistent instructional procedures.

Step 2: Collect Benchmarks of All Students' Performance Three Times during the School Year

Once an evidence-based instructional program has been implemented, the next step in RTI is to collect data on every student to learn which students are making effective progress and which ones need additional support. In the case of academic skills, curriculum-based measurement (CBM), including the Dynamic Indicators of Basic Early Literacy Skills (DIBELS), are well-researched evidence-based ways to document students' academic skills (Good & Kaminski, 2002; Shinn, 2005). Suggested time frames for collecting benchmark data have been developed for academic skills; these include the following:

Fall (September 15–October 15)
Winter (January 1–31)
Spring (May 1–31)

A number of specific planning activities are necessary to ensure that benchmark data are accurate and valid. To assist with such planning, blank benchmark planning worksheets are found in Forms 7.4 and 7.5 at the end of the chapter. Figures 7.3 and 7.4 depict completed worksheets used to plan and carry out the details of a benchmark process. These

Teacher's Name: _Mary Jones_____   Date: _10/12/04_ Time: _9:15–10:00___

Subject/Lesson: _Reading: Letter "B"_____   Evaluator: _X_ Self   Other: _____

Directions: The individual implementing this intervention is to complete this form at the end of every day regarding how they implemented the intervention during *that* day.

Intervention implemented by: __X__ Classroom teacher _____ Other: _____

Intervention Components	Completed		Comments
	Yes	No	
1. Handed out student materials.	X		
2. All students read all review words.		X	Peg was late to class and missed word review portion.
3. Immediate feedback given to students.	X		
4. Introduced new letter and sound, using script in teacher's manual.	X		
5. All students repeated new sound.		X	Alex was called to the office before practicing new sound.
6. Immediate feedback given to students.	X		
7. All students read story out loud.	X		
8. Each student correctly answered one question about story.		X	I forgot to call on Mark and Lynn.
9. All students produced three legible copies of letter of the day.	X		
10. Immediate feedback given to students.		X	Visitor came into classroom as I was giving feedback to students, and I skipped row 3 students.

FIGURE 7.2. Example of a completed Self-Report Treatment Integrity Assessment.

details include selecting and obtaining materials, training personnel and organizing materials for those who will collect benchmark data, working with students to collect benchmarks on stated days (including make-up days for absent students), managing the student database, and identifying which students need additional instruction (Burns, 2002).

Benchmark Materials

The best materials to use for benchmarking are curriculum-based measures. In the early days of CBM, all materials were created directly from the local curriculum. A large number of research studies showed that generic CBM materials work just as well as locally created items (Fuchs & Deno, 1994). For this reason, educators are encouraged to use

School/District: Riverview Elementary/Sunnyside District   Year: 2004–2005   Benchmark: (F) W S

Task	Person(s) Responsible	Deadline	Costs	Completed	Initials
Select materials for benchmarks.	Assessment Committee	March 1	none	Feb. 26	KPR
Obtain/copy needed materials.	Karen and Maria	June 1	$500	May 23	MRS
Make student name labels (if needed).	Not needed—teachers do	—	—	—	—
Train those collecting data.	David and Maria	Sept. 1	$150	Sept. 1	DSS
Organize/distribute materials.	Maria and Peggy	Sept. 15	none	Sept. 14	MRS
Collect benchmarks on stated dates.	K–2 teachers & students	Oct. 15	none	Oct. 9	MRS
Collect make-up benchmarks from absent students.	Maria and Peggy	Oct. 11	none	Oct. 11	MRS
Enter student scores into computer.	Peggy	Oct. 20	none	Oct 19	PHD
Create and distribute data summaries.	Maria and Peggy	Oct. 25	none	Oct 24	PHD
Identify students of concern.	Teachers and principals	Nov. 1	none	Oct 30	PHD

IMPLEMENT NEXT RTI STEP: TIER 2 INSTRUCTION

Notes: Need more clipboards for Winter benchmarks

FIGURE 7.3. Example of a completed Benchmark Planning Worksheet.

69

What	When	Who	Where	Materials Needed	Data Ready by
Fall Benchmarks	Oct. 1, 2, 3 9:10–11:30	All K–2 teachers and students; Title I staff and paraprofessionals	Kindergarten in Library Grade 1 in Gym Grade 2 in Cafeteria	CBM packet for each student Clipboards Stopwatches	October 25
Winter Benchmarks	Jan. 10, 11, 12 9:10–11:30	All K–2 teachers and students; Title I staff and paraprofessionals	Kindergarten in Library Grade 1 in Gym Grade 2 in Cafeteria	CBM packet for each student Clipboards Stopwatches	January 31
Spring Benchmarks	May 5, 6, 7 9:10–11:30	All K–2 teachers and students; Title I staff and paraprofessionals	Kindergarten in Library Grade 1 in Gym Grade 2 in Cafeteria	CBM packet for each students Clipboards Stopwatches	May 26

FIGURE 7.4. Example of a completed Benchmark Implementation Worksheet.

premade CBM items for benchmarking. Table 7.1 presents a summary of commercially available CBM materials as well as Internet sites where CBM materials can either be downloaded free or created using free online software. The largest and most empirically validated set of benchmark materials has been published by Edformation (2004). Edformation publishes reading and spelling benchmark probes for grades 1 through 8 and math benchmark probes for grades 1 through 6. In addition Edformation publishes preschool and kindergarten materials for early literacy and numeracy. All Edformation materials have been empirically validated for assessment of these basic skills. Edformation materials are available online, and purchasers may download and print what they need.

Another type of premade CBM materials for early literacy and reading are the Dynamic Indicators of Basic Early Literacy Skills. DIBELS for specific prereading skills are available for preschool through grade 1 students. DIBELS measures of oral reading are available for grades 1 through 6. DIBELS can be obtained in two different ways. These materials are available for free download at the DIBELS website (dibels.uoregon.edu). In addition, the same DIBELS items can be purchased in packaged sets from Sopris West. The two forms are very similar and measure the same skills.

For those schools who want more customized CBM items, there is a website where they can create their own materials for free. The site is www.interventioncentral.org and is a service of the Syracuse (New York) public schools. At the site there are a number of CBM tools, including software applications for creating both reading and math CBM

TABLE 7.1. Summary of Published Curriculum-Based Measurement Materials

Publisher	Web address	Materials	Grades
Edformation	www.edformation.com	Early Literacy Reading:	Preschool–1
		Oral	1–8
		Silent (maze)	1–8
		Spelling	1–8
		Early Numeracy	Preschool–1
		Math	1–6
DIBELS[a]	dibels.uoregon.edu	Early Literacy Reading:	Preschool–1
		Oral	1–6
Sopris West[b]	www.sopriswest.com	Early Literacy Reading:	Preschool–1
		Oral	1–6
Information Central[a]	www.interventioncentral.org	Reading software:	1–12
		Oral	
		Math software	1–6
Pro-Ed	www.pro-ed.com	Measuring Basic Skills Program (Macintosh computer program) for:	
		Reading	1–6
		Math	1–6

[a] All materials at this site can be downloaded and used for free.
[b] Sopris West has the exclusive rights to sell packaged versions of all the DIBELS materials.

items. The reading probe generator creates oral reading fluency probes from text that is entered by the user. Probes can be created from literature or expository texts. The reading software also calculates the readability level of each probe generated. Intervention Central also includes a math probe generator. This software allows users to create math computation probes for addition, subtraction, multiplication, and division. Users can choose how many problems will be on each page, what type of skill the problems will measure (e.g., adding sums to 18), and how big the font size will be. Both the reading software and math software generate a student copy and a teacher copy for every probe created. The Intervention Central site includes links to a number of other CBM tools, including free literature-based silent-reading probes for grades 4–6, CBM manuals for teachers, and graphing tools.

Pro-Ed Publishing sells a Macintosh computer CBM software for reading and math. This software is for computer-based testing only, so students must be at an individual computer station to use it. The software covers math and reading skills for grades 1–6. The software provides immediate corrective feedback to the student and includes graphs of student progress over time. The students' scores are summarized in teacher reports that show which students made progress and which ones did not.

Another important aspect of the benchmarking process is data management. In order for the data collected from the benchmarks to be maximally useful, they need to be organized and shared in systematic ways. At a minimum, the students' scores need to be entered into some form of database. The simplest form of such a database is paper-based. Student data can be summarized by simply rank ordering the students according to their scores. Most schools which have utilized RTI methods have chosen to enter their benchmark scores into some form of computer database. There are a variety of hardware and software tools available for schools to use to manage benchmark data. Although there are many manufacturers of these products, they can be grouped into two types: stand-alone and network-based.

Stand-Alone Data Management

Benchmark data can be entered into one stand-alone computer workstation. The chosen computer could run any type of operating system, including Apple (Macintosh), Windows, UNIX, or others. The important feature of the computer is that data management software be installed on it. Examples of such software include Microsoft Excel, Claris Works, and others. If the school has specialized data management software for other student information such as attendance, grades, and assessment, the benchmark data can probably be entered into that data set instead of into a separate file. It is ideal to have all student data in one common place so that information about students is centralized and important related data can be simultaneously retrieved and reviewed. If the benchmark data are housed on one computer, it is *essential* that the data file(s) be backed up on a regular basis. The downside to using only one computer workstation to store the data is that, were the computer or file damaged, the data would be lost. For this reason, it may be better to store and manage the data on a computer network.

Network Data Management

An alternative to using one computer to store benchmark data is to use a computer network in which the data are stored on a central server but can be accessed by many people through computers on the network. There are a number of benefits to managing benchmark data on a computer network. First, the way that computer networks are set up and managed includes regular data backups and multiple storage locations; this means that the benchmark data are less vulnerable to loss if the computer is damaged. Second, when data can be accessed from a number of locations, many people who need access to the data can obtain it quickly and easily for instructional decision making. Finally, the type of network used may enhance the nature of the benchmark reports and offer multiple ways to display the data. For example, data can be displayed for an entire grade or class or for an individual student.

There are several Internet-based benchmark data services that offer flexible ways to manage student information. All of these data services must be purchased by the school or district, and the rates are set and vary according to each service provider. There is a data service that accompanies the DIBELS that is set up to provide group and individual score reports specifically for all DIBELS measures. This service can be used only with DIBELS data, but is fast and less expensive than some other service providers. AIMSweb is a data management service system that allows for data from a number of academic skills measures; it is owned and run by Edformation. Through Edformation, AIMSWeb has its own set of CBM benchmark measures but can also accommodate data entry of other measures as well. AIMSWeb also has an RTI-specific data management tool for managing students' scores as they move between different stages of RTI. The critical feature of the data management system used to support RTI activities is that it be sustainable over time for the types of data used (see Box 7.1).

Step 3: Identify Which Students Scored below the Benchmark Target(s)

Once benchmark data are organized, they can be used to review and identify which students are not meeting the goals. A two-part process of reviewing student data is recommended. The first part includes comparing the scores obtained by all students with national benchmarks. Such benchmarks are not necessarily available for all skills; however, when available, national benchmarks are a good starting point because they can shed light on whether a school's performance levels are in line with national trends. Both the DIBELS and Edformation websites have continuously updated national norms for their measures. Table 7.2 shows national norms for second graders' scores on oral reading fluency. Compare these scores with those shown in Table 7.3 for a few second-grade students. Those students with low scores need to be considered at risk for reading problems.

The second part of data review involves comparing individual student performance with the average performance of all the students in the same grade. This process is made easier if the students' scores are organized according to percentiles so that those students scoring at or below a specific percentile rank are reviewed in detail. Researchers have

BOX 7.1. Creating Cool Graphs of Student Data

All of the graphs of student data in this book were created using Microsoft Graph, which is part of the Office software suite. To create graphs like ours do the following:

1. Open Microsoft (MS) Word.
2. Click on the "Insert" menu item.
3. Highlight and click on "Object . . ."
4. A dialogue box will appear in which you can select what to insert.
5. Scroll down the right side of the box and locate "Microsoft Graph Chart."
6. Click on "Microsoft Graph Chart," then click on "OK."
7. A set of new windows will appear on your screen. One will be the graph, and another is the datasheet into which the graph values are entered. Both will appear with pre-entered sample data.
8. Click on the first column of the datasheet, and change the value to reflect your data. If you have more than one dependent variable to graph, change the next row of data, and so forth, until all desired values are entered.
9. Click the upper-right "go away" box on the datasheet.
10. Click once in the white area of the graph, then right-click your mouse to open a command box. In this box highlight and click on "Chart Type . . . "
11. A new dialogue box will open. In the left side of the box click on the preferred chart type (probably "line").
12. After selecting the chart type, choose the chart subtype from the box on the right-hand side of the dialogue box. We use the first type in the middle row, described as a "line with markers displayed at each data value."
13. Click OK to select this chart type. Note that you can set this format as your default chart type by clicking this box before closing the dialogue box.
14. The chart should appear with your data. You can change the size of the chart in your document by clicking and dragging the corner/side arrows.
15. You can edit every part of the chart by right-clicking on any part of the chart and entering new values in the dialogue box for that feature.

TABLE 7.2. Oral Reading Fluency National Norms for Second-Grade Students

Percentile	Fall	Winter	Spring
90	99	121	139
75	73	97	114
50	49	69	86
25	24	40	59
10	14	18	27

Note. From Edformation (2004). Reprinted by permission.

TABLE 7.3. Fall Oral Reading Fluency Scores and Percentile Ranks for Second-Grade Students

Student	ORF score	Percentile rank
Brown, Ben	84	87
Martin, Steve	12	9
Reynolds, Gail	51	50
Wilson, Martha	16	16

looked at different "cut points" or percentile ranks as starting points for reviewing individual student scores. The range of percentile ranks that usually serve as starting points for reviewing student's scores are the 16th to 25th. The 25th percentile roughly approximates the low end of the average range of scores and offers an inclusive starting point for reviewing data. The 16th percentile represents the bottom end of one standard deviation from the overall average score. It is not so important what percentile rank is chosen as the starting point; rather, it is the process of reviewing the data for all students below a certain rank that is critical. In time, once a series of scores for students is entered and reviewed, appropriate local cut-scores for starting the process of determining which students are at risk for significant school problems can be set for each benchmark measure used.

The process of reviewing those students who score at and below a certain score allows teachers to consider each student's overall skill development in each area of concern. This process can be facilitated with the Instruction Planning Worksheet. A blank worksheet is shown in Form 7.6 (at the end of the chapter), and a sample completed one is shown in Figure 7.5. This worksheet provides spaces for entering the name of each student at risk as well as the specific nature of the current instructional needs. This is important because not all at-risk students will have the same needs. For example, in the area of reading, some students may need to learn sound–symbol correspondence while others need to work on reading more quickly (fluency). By listing each student at risk, the teacher can consider what the exact instructional needs are and create instructional groupings that match the student's needs. Sometimes, a student's instructional needs will not be clear from benchmark data alone. Teachers need to consider other data they have about a student's performance alongside the benchmark scores. If needed, additional brief testing with other CBM measures may help shed light on the student's current needs (Shinn, 1989, 1998).

Step 4: Provide Daily Scientifically Based Small-Group Instruction

After identifying which students are not meeting the benchmarks, RTI procedures involve providing those students with additional evidence-based instruction. For example, in the area of math, those students not meeting a grade 1 winter benchmark of adding two single-digit numbers should be given additional daily instruction in adding single digits up to a sum of 10. In order to know what small-group (Tier 2) instructional methods or programs are likely to help these students, a review of available materials is needed. As

Student	Describe Instructional Need	Instructional Methods to Be Tried	Progress Monitoring Measure	Program Start Date	Review Progress Date	Person Responsible
Smith, Mary	Segment words orally	Early Reading Intervention (ERI)	PSF	Nov. 3	Nov. 29	PHD
Gray, Billy	Blend words while reading	Project Read	NWF	Oct. 29	Nov. 29	MRS
Cohen, Nick	Read more quickly	Great Leaps	ORF	Nov. 5	Nov. 29	MRS
White, Polly	Segment words orally	Early Reading Intervention (ERI)	PSF	Nov. 4	Nov. 29	PHD
O'Reilly, Mark	Match sounds to letters	Sound Partners	NWF	Nov. 5	Nov. 29	PHD
Webber, Karl	Match sounds to letters	Sound Partners	NWF	Nov. 3	Nov. 29	PHD
Gage, Robin	Number identification	Touch Math	CBM-M 100	Nov. 4	Nov. 30	KPT
Plummer, Max	Number identification	Touch math	CBM-M-100	Oct. 30	Nov. 30	KPT
Silver, Duane	Adding single digits, no regrouping	Great Leaps Math	CBM-M	Nov. 2	Nov. 30	EBC
Black, Melissa	Adding digits w/regrouping	Great Leaps Math	CBM-M	Nov. 5	Nov. 30	EBC
Boxer, Fred	Adding single digits, no regrouping	Great Leaps Math	CBM-M	Nov. 4	Nov. 30	EBC

FIGURE 7.5. Example of a completed Tier 2 Instruction Planning Worksheet.

with Tier 1 interventions, evidence for the efficacy of Tier 2 interventions needs to be reviewed. A blank worksheet for summarizing evidence supporting the effectiveness of possible Tier 2 interventions is presented as Form 7.7 (at the end of the chapter), and Figure 7.6 a completed Small-Group Instructional Materials Review Worksheet. This worksheet allows comparison of specific programs and the research validating their efficacy. In the case of math, far fewer research studies have documented which programs work better than others. The one empirically validated program listed is Touch Math, which has been found to help some students in developing basic math skills.

Another, newer, program that holds promise is Great Leaps Math (2004). Although scientific research about this program is not yet available, it was developed by the same research team that created Great Leaps Reading. The reading program does have strong empirical support, so the math program is likely to have features based on scientific principles. In cases where scientific research about a program is not yet published, educators may have to make selections on the basis of prior work by the same research team or other program features associated with scientifically based instructional practices. Once a program of instruction has been selected, it should be used until one of two outcomes occurs: either the student reaches the math benchmark and no longer needs additional assistance, or the small-group sessions yield data indicating that the intervention is not working and another intervention is tried.

While specific guidelines for how long to implement Tier 2 interventions are still being developed, other principles of data collection and management can be applied to help educators know when to discontinue an intervention. As noted in Form 7.1, Tier 2 activities should be tried for at least 3 weeks, with data about student performance collected at least once per week. This guideline is based on evidence that a minimum of three data points are needed to determine if there is any trend in the outcomes (Steege et al., 2002). Pragmatic considerations need to be used as well. Given the variability in daily routines in most school settings, it is likely that there will be some days when the math instruction cannot be fully implemented. It is important that any intervention be tried long enough for changes in student performance to be possible.

Forms 7.8 and 7.9 are blank worksheets designed to help teachers know when an intervention is working and when something else should be tried. Figure 7.7 is a completed Tier 2 Instructional Methods Teacher Log. It includes notes from a Tier 2 small-group teacher who worked with students needing help with reading skills. The student described in Figure 7.7 is Nick Sweet. This page of the teacher's log records his teacher's judgment that he is not making much progress. Figure 7.8 shows Nick's data for 3 weeks of general education instruction (9/17–9/30 plottings), as well as scores from 3 weeks when an empirically based small-group program (Sounds Sense) was used. This graph confirms his teacher's perception: Nick made little progress in decoding nonsense words as measured by weekly DIBELS after the program began. Of note, if the intervention were used for only 1 or 2 weeks, student progress might not be noticeable. However, there is an upper limit to how long an intervention should be used if the data suggest it is not working. No intervention should be continued for more than 6 weeks if the data indicate that the student is not making improvement. In cases when the daily assessment data suggest that a student is not making progress, the Tier 2 activities should be changed

Program (Publisher and date)	Knowledge and Skills Covered in Program	Program Age/Grade	Research Evidence Supporting Program	How Is Student Progress in Program Monitored?	Costs (w/ training)
Touch Math (Innovative Learning Concepts, 2004)	Number Identification, Quantity, Basic Operations	K–2	Scott, K. S. (1993). Multisensory mathematics for children with mild disabilities. Exceptionality, 4 (2), 97–111. Showed greater gains for students in Touch Math group.	Not specified	$609 (for first grade kit)
Great Leaps Math (Great Leaps, 2003)	Computation Fluency	K–4	No research found	Increased fluency on daily probes included with program	$275
Schoolhouse Mathematics Laboratory (SRA, 2000)	Number Identification, Computation Fluency, Applied problems	1–3	No research found	Built-in skill checks	$535

FIGURE 7.6. Example of a completed Small-Group Instructional Materials Review Worksheet.

Teacher: ___Mary Poppins___   Student: ___Nick Sweet___

Date/Time	Teaching Activities Used	Rating	Ideas for Next Session
Monday, October 17	Introduced sound for letter n by telling students sound, having students rehearse /n/ sound 5 times, identify n in words, and practicing /n/ in short words of known letters and sounds (on, un, in).	4	Nick did not quickly identify /n/ in the practice words; he appeared to need more practice locating /n/ in words. Next time I will have him practice with 10 words.
Tuesday, October 18	We did a round-robin word read first. Each student read a word while the other students watched. Each time the set of 10 words was read a new student started so that every student read each word. We finished with a story with the words.	5	Heavy practice seems to make a big difference for Nick, so I plan to do more cumulative review lessons in the future.
Wednesday, October 19	Introduced sound for long /ō/ by telling students sound, having student rehearse /ō/ sound 10 times, identify /ō/ in silent e words. Did rhyming with /ō/ words, each student generating a new rhymed word.	3	Nick was not very engaged today and seemed hesitant with rhyming activity. I will alter that activity so that I generate the rhyme word and the students say it.
Thursday, October 20	Reviewed long /ō/ and taught words with silent e and /ō/; had students practice each word then use it in a sentence. Students made up an oral story using long /ō/ words. I read them a story with /ō/ words in it.	2	I am worried that Nick is becoming less engaged in each session. He seems hesitant to respond, even when he knows the answers. He says "I don't know" often. I will DIBEL him tomorrow.
Friday, October 21	Did Nonsense Word Fluency with all kids today. Many are making great progress. Appears to be time for regrouping students.	4	Nick got a 25 on NWF today, no gain since his last score. He is not making much progress in the 4-student group, so I'm going to switch him to 2:1 for 3 weeks and see if that helps.

Teacher rating (1–5) of effectiveness of teaching session, with 1 = very low and 5 = very high.

FIGURE 7.7. Example of a completed Tier 2 Instructional Methods Teacher Log.

79

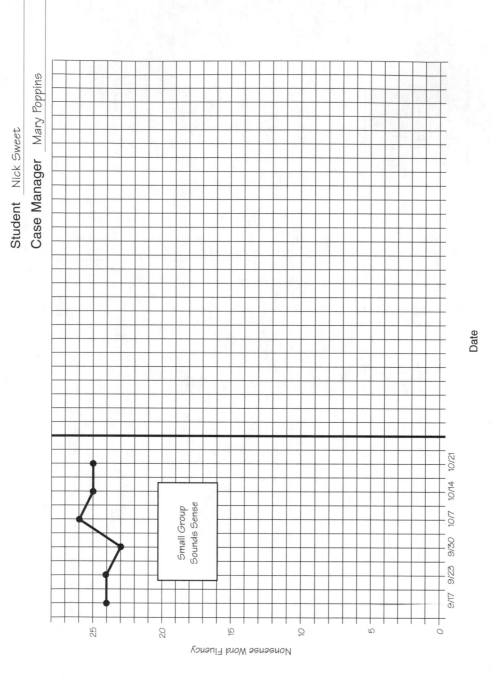

Student Nick Sweet

Case Manager Mary Poppins

Nonsense Word Fluency

Small Group
Sounds Sense

Date

FIGURE 7.8. Example of a completed Progress Monitoring Graph.

or replaced with another level of intervention, which should then be implemented for at least 3 weeks but not more than 6 weeks if no progress is seen.

Form 7.9 and Figure 7.9, respectively, show blank and completed Student Progress Review Worksheets. This worksheet allows the teacher to review specific questions about a student's progress and make decisions based on the data. In this case, over the 6 weeks of instruction (Tiers 1 and 2) Nick had only one data point showing improvement and four data points showing no progress. Based on these data, his teacher decided to change his program. Starting on October 23 she switched him to a smaller group with two students. Nick's progress in the new grouping will be reviewed later in this chapter. Importantly, his teacher set a specific date to review his program again.

Step 5: Monitor Student Progress toward the Benchmark(s), Using Frequent Assessments

Importantly, the students who participate in Tier 2 instruction need to be assessed regularly. This is important for two reasons. First, frequent feedback on performance has been shown to enhance student progress. Second, only by collecting daily feedback will the student and teacher know if the additional instruction is yielding the desired goal of improving the students' skills. The nature of data to be collected should be decided at the time the intervention is developed. In some cases, intervention programs come with daily assessment tools. For example, Great Leaps for reading and math includes daily assessment as part of the sessions, and progress monitoring charts are included in the kits. Progress monitoring assessment items have been developed for basic reading, spelling, and math skills. The DIBELS system has progress monitoring forms for all DIBELS tasks, including oral reading fluency, in English and Spanish (Good & Kaminski, 2002). The AIMSweb data management system includes progress monitoring items for purchase, as well (Edformation, 2004). Alternatively, teachers can develop their own assessment and monitoring tools by using the software at www.interventioncentral.org. There are two critical features that need to be integrated in progress monitoring assessments. First, they need to involve performance of exactly the same skills as those being taught in the intervention. Second, there need to be at least 20 forms of the items so that different forms can be used (so students will not memorize the answers).

In addition to the progress monitoring items themselves, teachers will want to have a graph on which student assessment data can be recorded each day. A reproducible graph for such purposes is found in Form 7.10. This graph has equal intervals across both the X and Y axes, and the student or teacher can fill in the numbers for the Y axis and dates on the X axis. Sample completed graphs are shown in Figures 7.8 and 7.10. Ideally, students should fill in their own data because it saves time for the teacher and helps students be in tune with their own skill performance. Progress monitoring data should be collected at least once per week and more often in cases where a student is receiving more intensive instruction. In cases where the student is able to handle it, he or she and the teacher can conduct a brief error analysis to identify what skill(s) are improving the most and what one(s) still need more learning and practice. Such performance reviews should be used to determine the content, order, and frequency of subsequent Tier 2 lessons.

Student: _Nick Sweet_   Grade: 1   Teacher: _Mary Poppins_

Name of Tier 2 instruction program: _Sounds Sense_

Who is the teacher? _Mary Poppins_

How many students (total) are in the instruction group? _4_

How often are the instructional sessions held? _Daily_

How long is each session? _30 minutes_

How many sessions has this student attended? _27 out of 30_

Based on the progress-monitoring data, how many data points indicate that the student's skills are improving? _1_

DECISION RULE: IF THE STUDENT HAS 3 OR MORE DATA POINTS SHOWING IMPROVEMENT, MAINTAIN THE PROGRAM

Based on the progress-monitoring data, how many data points indicate that the student's skills are not improving? _4_

DECISION RULE: IF THE STUDENT HAS 3 OR MORE DATA POINTS SHOWING NO IMPROVEMENT, CHANGE THE PROGRAM

How do the student's current skills compare to typically achieving peers? _Nick's current score of 25 is below the minimum benchmark of 30 for midyear grade 1 students_

DECISION RULE: IF THE STUDENT HAS 6 OR MORE DATA POINTS SHOWING PERFORMANCE AT GRADE LEVEL, DISCONTINUE INTERVENTION

Based on the obtained data, what modifications to the current instructional program will be made? _Nick has not made effective progress in Sounds Sense in the last 3 weeks. I will begin 2:1 daily sessions with Nick and another student to see if a smaller group helps improve his reading._

When will the modifications go into effect? _Monday, October 24_

When will the student's progress be reviewed again? _Friday, November 11_

ALL PROGRESS-MONITORING DATA AND GRAPHS REFERENCED ABOVE MUST BE ATTACHED

Person completing this form: _Mary Poppins, MEd_   Date: _October 21, 2005_

FIGURE 7.9. Example of a completed Student Progress Review Worksheet.

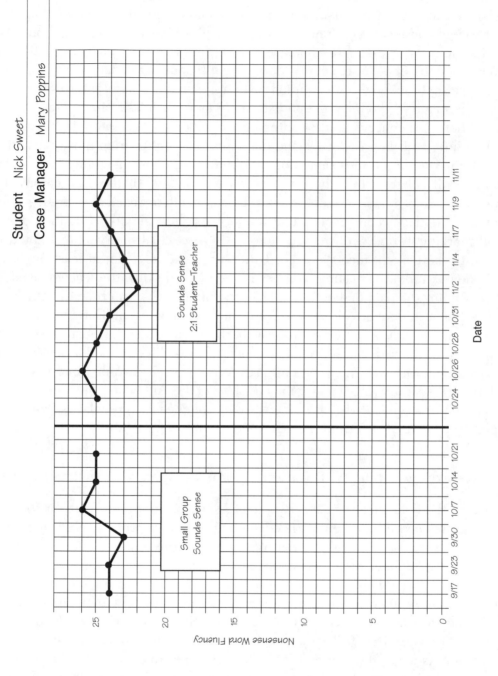

Student _Nick Sweet_

Case Manager _Mary Poppins_

Nonsense Word Fluency

Small Group
Sounds Sense

Sounds Sense
2:1 Student–Teacher

Date

FIGURE 7.10. Example of a completed Progress Monitoring Graph.

83

Step 6: Review, Revise, and/or Discontinue Small-Group Instruction

Once at least 3 weeks of data are collected about a student's skill performance, the graph can be reviewed to determine what the next step should be. As discussed in Chapter 5, the easiest way to conduct such a review is to use single-subject research methods. The first step in such a process is to compare the student's performance from the pre-intervention stage (baseline) to the intervention stage. If none of the data points collected during each phase (baseline vs. intervention) overlap, then meaningful interpretations of the data can be made. If the intervention data share more than 20% of overlapping data points, then there is a concern that the intervention data are not meaningfully different from the baseline data. In cases when the data points do not overlap more often than 20%, if at all, intervention trends should be reviewed. Data showing an improvement in the student's skill suggests that the intervention is working. In these situations, the teacher needs to determine how soon the student is likely to reach the target performance level. If the data trend suggests that the target skill level will be attained during the current marking period with the intervention in place, that intervention should be continued until the student meets or exceeds the target skill level for at least 3 weeks.

Even when a student is making progress in the desired skills, the teacher needs to continually monitor the data to determine when the intervention can be reduced or discontinued. When a student has obtained three or more data points indicating grade-level performance on the skill, an intervention can be reduced or discontinued. Usually an intervention should be reduced in frequency before being discontinued altogether. For example, a student who was receiving daily sessions could get two or three sessions a week with progress monitoring showing maintenance of the skill before the Tier 2 lessons are discontinued. In each of these cases, it is the data obtained from regular assessment of student performance that determines the next course of action.

Step 7: Increase the Intensity, Duration, and/or Frequency of Instruction

In cases where the data suggest that the student's skills are not improving, or they are getting worse, the current intervention needs to be changed or replaced. In some cases, intervention changes could include increasing the amount of time for intervention sessions, reducing the number of students participating in the sessions, or increasing the number of times the student practices the target skill during the intervention. If the teacher believes that such changes to the intervention are not likely to enhance the student's skills, then at least one more intervention should be tried before moving on to the next stage of RTI procedures. In Nick's case, his teacher decided to try teaching sessions with fewer students to see if the opportunity for Nick to respond more often in each session would help his reading skills. Progress data for this new intervention are found in Figure 7.10.

As soon as the new intervention is implemented, the change in the instructional format needs to be noted on the progress monitoring graph. This can be done by drawing a vertical line at the point in the graph when the intervention changed (see Figure 7.10). Then, new progress-monitoring data can be recorded on the same graph as the old data, and comparisons between the interventions can be made. *Any* changes in the intervention need to be noted on the graph with a vertical line. Even slight changes such as the length of sessions must be recorded so that the methodological differences between the interventions can be noted.

Step 8: Review, Revise, and/or Discontinue Small-Group Instruction

As shown in Figure 7.10, Nick did not make any gains when the sessions included just two students. His scores on nonsense word fluency did not improve under the new conditions. As a result of these data, Nick's teacher decided to refer him for evaluation for special education. In order to take advantage of the data collected during the Tier 2 phases of the RTI process, this information can be summarized and shared in the special education referral form. Form 7.11 (at the end of the chapter) is a blank referral form, and Figure 7.11 shows a sample completed referral form. Some states and school districts have their own referral forms; however, these data could be attached or integrated with those forms. Importantly, this form provides information about the type, duration, frequency, and intensity of instruction used to help the student. As explained in Chapter 3, IDEIA 2004 allows such data to be used as part of the evaluation procedures for determining whether a student has a disability.

Step 9: Comprehensive Evaluation, If Needed

What about situations in which the student does not make progress despite use of several evidence-based interventions? When the best efforts to help a student succeed in school do not yield the desired gains, and the student is still not making overall progress, the student should be referred for a comprehensive evaluation for special education eligibility. As noted in Chapter 2, RTI methods are included in both NCLB and IDEIA 2004 as part of special eligibility decision making. In other words, schools need to try to meet a student's learning needs before referring a student to special education. Those students who are not successful in school despite the use of evidence-based instruction at Tier 1 and Tier 2 of the RTI model may have significant and chronic needs that are best met with more specialized educational services. Not all comprehensive evaluations are the same. As outlined in IDEIA 2004, the evaluation procedures need to take into account the specific presenting needs of the student as well as the data collected as part of RTI procedures. The goal of the evaluation process is to identify and define the specific nature of the student's difficulties in school.

Step 10: Special Education Eligibility

If, as a result of the comprehensive evaluation, it is determined by the special education team that a student is eligible for special education services, the team will then need to develop an IEP that includes evidence-based instruction to meet the student's needs. Specific details about how to conduct a comprehensive evaluation based on RTI principles are found in Chapters 9 and 10. Some students may be eligible for special education

Student: Nick Sweet   **Grade:** 1   **Teacher:** Mary Poppins

Describe how student's instructional need was initially identified:

Nick scored in the at-risk range on the kindergarten DIBELS at every benchmark period last year.

Tier 2 instructional methods that were used to improve student's knowledge/skills:

3 weeks of small-group Sounds Sense lessons with 4–5 students in group followed by 3 weeks of Sounds Sense Lessons with 2 students in group. Lessons covered sound–symbol mapping, practicing learned sounds in real and nonsense words, and reading short stories composed of learned words.

Who provided the Tier 2 instructional program?

Mary Poppins, Certified Highly Qualified Special Education Teacher

Progress-monitoring measure used to record student's progress during Tier 2 instruction:

Nonsense word fluency of DIBELS

Tier 2 program start date: *October 3*   **Tier 2 program review date(s):** *October 21, November 11*

Describe the student's current instructional need(s):

Nick needs to learn sound–symbol correspondence and master the alphabetic principle. He can decode a few words using this principle, but has not mastered all letter sounds.

What, if any, additional instruction or supports is this student currently receiving?

Nick is receiving 30 minutes per day of Sounds Sense 2:1 instruction until a comprehensive evaluation can be completed.

ALL PROGRESS-MONITORING DATA AND GRAPHS REFERENCED ABOVE MUST BE ATTACHED

Person completing this form: *Mary Poppins, MEd*   **Date:** *November 11, 2005*

FIGURE 7.11. Example of a completed Tier 3 Referral for Special Education Worksheet.

and receive all instruction through special education, whereas others may participate in both general and special education programs. In all cases, student progress needs to be monitored frequently so that the effectiveness of the instruction is documented and changes to programs based on data can be provided.

SUMMARY

This chapter has provided a comprehensive discussion of the steps included in RTI practices. There are 10 possible steps that educators need to consider when implementing RTI procedures in schools. Not all students will need all 10 steps. The worksheet forms included in the chapter offer educators tools to develop their own skills for utilizing RTI methods. Teachers may choose to customize the worksheets and procedures described here. So long as the instructional methods are scientifically based and accurate data about student progress are collected frequently, local adaptations of RTI are likely to yield beneficial results for all students.

FORM 7.1.

RTI IMPLEMENTATION CHECKLIST

Check   RTI steps

_____

1. Implement scientifically based general education instructional methods.

    _____ Verify accuracy of instructional procedures with integrity assessment.

_____

2. Collect benchmarks of all students' performance three times during the school year.

_____

3. Identify which students scored below the benchmark target(s).

_____

4. Provide daily scientifically based small-group instruction to students with scores below benchmark target(s) for at least 3 weeks.

    _____ Verify accuracy of instructional procedures with integrity assessment.

_____

5. Monitor student progress toward the benchmark(s), using daily assessments and data graphing for 3 school weeks.

_____

6. Review, revise, and/or discontinue small-group instruction based on student performance and progress toward the benchmark at the end of 3 weeks.

_____

7. For students not yet showing evidence of progress toward meeting the benchmark(s) by the end of the first 3 weeks, increase the intensity, duration, and/or frequency of instruction and continue to monitor progress for up to another 3 weeks.

_____

8. Review, revise, and/or discontinue small-group instruction, based on student performance and attainment of benchmark at the end of the second 3 weeks.

_____

9. For students not yet showing evidence of meeting the benchmark(s) by the end of the school year, initiate a comprehensive evaluation to determine whether the student has a disability and is eligible for special education services.

_____

10. IEP team determines whether student has a disability and meets the criteria for special education services; if the student is eligible for special education, an IEP is developed and becomes the student's new instructional program.

INSTRUCTIONAL MATERIALS REVIEW WORKSHEET

Program	Publisher (Date)	Research Evidence	Connections to Local Goals	Observations

FORM 7.3.

TREATMENT INTEGRITY CHECKLIST

Teacher's Name: _____   Date: _____   Time: _____

Subject/Lesson: _____   Evaluator: Self   Other: _____

Directions: The individual implementing this intervention is to complete this form at the end of every day regarding how they implemented the intervention during *that* day.

Intervention implemented by: ____ Classroom teacher _____ Other: _____

Intervention Components	Completed		Comments
	Yes	No	

FORM 7.4.

BENCHMARK PLANNING WORKSHEET

School/District: _____ Year: _____ Benchmark: F W S

Task	Person(s) Responsible	Deadline	Costs	Completed	Initials
Select materials for benchmarks					
Obtain/copy needed materials					
Make student name labels (if needed)					
Train those collecting data					
Organize/distribute materials					
Collect benchmarks on stated dates					
Collect make-up benchmarks from absent students					
Enter student scores into computer					
Create and distribute data summaries					
Identify students of concern					
IMPLEMENT NEXT RTI STEP: TIER 2 INSTRUCTION					

Notes:

BENCHMARK IMPLEMENTATION WORKSHEET

What	When	Who	Where	Materials Needed	Data Ready by
Fall Benchmarks					
Winter Benchmarks					
Spring Benchmarks					

FORM 7.6.

TIER 2 INSTRUCTION PLANNING WORKSHEET

Student	Describe Instructional Need	Instructional Methods to Be Tried	Progress Monitoring Measure	Program Start Date	Progress Review Date	Person Responsible

SMALL-GROUP INSTRUCTIONAL MATERIALS REVIEW WORKSHEET

Program (publisher and date)	Knowledge and Skills Covered in Program	Program Age/Grade	Research Evidence Supporting Program	How Is Student Progress in Program Monitored?	Costs (w/training)

FORM 7.8.

TIER 2 INSTRUCTIONAL METHODS TEACHER LOG

Teacher: _____   Student: _____

Date/Time	Teaching Activities Used	Rating	Ideas for Next Session

*Teacher rating (1–5) of effectiveness of teaching session, with 1 = very low and 5 = very high.

STUDENT PROGRESS REVIEW WORKSHEET

Student:	Grade:	Teacher:

Name of Tier 2 instruction program:
Who is the teacher?
How many students (total) are in the instruction group?
How often are the instructional sessions held?
How long is each session?
How many sessions has this student attended?
Based on the progress-monitoring data, how many data points indicate that the student's skills are improving?
DECISION RULE: IF THE STUDENT HAS 3 OR MORE DATA POINTS SHOWING IMPROVEMENT, MAINTAIN THE PROGRAM
Based on the progress-monitoring data, how many data points indicate that the student's skills are not improving?
DECISION RULE: IF THE STUDENT HAS 3 OR MORE DATA POINTS SHOWING NO IMPROVEMENT, CHANGE THE PROGRAM
How do the student's current skills compare to typically achieving peers?
DECISION RULE: IF THE STUDENT HAS 6 OR MORE DATA POINTS SHOWING PERFORMANCE AT GRADE LEVEL, DISCONTINUE INTERVENTION
Based on the obtained data, what modifications to the current instructional program will be made?
When will the modifications go into effect?
When will the student's progress be reviewed again?
ALL PROGRESS-MONITORING DATA AND GRAPHS REFERENCED ABOVE MUST BE ATTACHED

Person completing this form:	Date:

FORM 7.10.

PROGRESS MONITORING GRAPH

Student _____

Case Manager _____

Date

TIER 3 REFERRAL
FOR SPECIAL EDUCATION WORKSHEET

Student: _____ Grade: _____ Teacher: _____

Describe how student's instructional need was initially identified:
Tier 2 instructional methods that were used to improve student's knowledge/skills:
Who provided the Tier 2 instructional program?
Progress-monitoring measure used to record student's progress during Tier 2 instruction:
Tier 2 program start date: _____ Tier 2 program review date(s):
Describe the student's current instructional need(s):
What, if any, additional instruction or supports is this student currently receiving?
ALL PROGRESS-MONITORING DATA AND GRAPHS REFERENCED ABOVE MUST BE ATTACHED
Person completing this form: _____ Date:

8

Using RTI Procedures with Students from Diverse Backgrounds

Considering Ability, Culture, Language, Race, and Religion

DIVERSE STUDENT BACKGROUNDS AND NEEDS

Students in U.S. schools come from a wide variety of backgrounds (National Center for Education Statistics, 2004). In some areas of the United States, the majority of students speak Spanish (or another language). Many students have distinct racial, cultural, ability, and religious identities that are different from dominant U.S. traditions. As a result of these unique backgrounds, some students may enter school with expectations and beliefs other than those held by their teachers. Indeed, although the population of school students is becoming increasingly diverse, the demographic profile of U.S. teachers remains primarily English-speaking and Caucasian (National Center for Education Statistics, 2004). One of the possible outcomes from such differences in student and teacher backgrounds is that students may feel misunderstood by their teachers (Cartledge, 1996). Although RTI procedures are designed so they can be used with students from a wide variety of backgrounds and experiences, it is important that educators take into account the unique qualities of all students when using RTI methods. This chapter will provide a discussion and explanation of how RTI steps can be used with students who possess a wide variety of abilities and cultural, linguistic, racial, and religious identities.

The diversity of backgrounds among U.S. families means that not all students may be expecting the same thing from their school experiences (Boscardin, Brown-Chidsey, & Gonzalez-Martinez, 2002a). For example, a student whose parents immigrated to the United States for the purpose of providing their children with a better education may start school with a different mindset than one whose parents had limited and negative school encounters during their own childhoods. While each family will have certain characteristics that are unique, there are some features that can be used to understand the school expectations of students and their families. Below we discuss five key features of students' backgrounds that are likely to influence their school expectations and experiences: ability, culture, language, race, and religion.

Ability

Ability is a loose and generic term that we have chosen to describe features about an individual student's early childhood that relate to all domains of human development. The converse of ability is *dis*ability. The term *disability* is widely used to refer to developmental conditions that affect all aspects of a person's life. Still, the term disability has a negative connotation, thus, we have chosen to use the term *ability* instead. By ability, we mean the person-specific characteristics and features that influence school experiences and performance. For example, a student with cerebral palsy may or may not have muscular or orthopedic difficulties that could influence school activities. Similarly, a student with autism could have person-specific behaviors that affect interpersonal communications. By using the term ability, we want to focus on what the student *can* do, not what he or she cannot do. By the time a student enters school, specific ability-related experiences are likely to have shaped his or her learning history. These experiences may have an effect on the student's and her family's expectations about school.

In the case of certain conditions such as hearing impairment, blindness, autism, and genetic abnormalities, a student's specific and unique abilities and limitations will have been identified long before school entry (Brown & Brown, 2005). Indeed, there is a huge benefit to early identification and intervention for many such conditions (Bagnato & Neisworth, 1991). For example, in the case of hearing impairment or deafness, it is likely that a student's family will have already made certain key decisions about the communication instruction desired for the student. This instruction could include using American Sign Language (ASL), Signed Exact English (SEE), oral language training, hearing aids, or a combination of all these approaches. For students with hearing loss, the choice of communication instruction begins well before kindergarten but will have a lasting impact of all future schooling. Similarly, for students with conditions identified at birth and early childhood, at the time of school entry the history of past interventions must be taken into account. The student's early childhood interventions and experiences with them will influence expectations and goals for subsequent school performance.

Other students may have ability features that are not detected until the time of formal school entry. This is one of the reasons for *child find* requirements and activities. Child find is a provision of IDEIA 2004 that requires all public school entities, as well as preschool intervention programs for students ages 3 to 5, to locate and assist any and all students with developmental needs prior to kindergarten. The goal of child find is to identify and provide interventions for students who would benefit from early intervention services. Kindergarten screening procedures are part of child find activities because they offer a way to review the ability profiles of all students when they enter formal schooling at age 5. In some cases, students with developmental ability needs are not identified until the kindergarten screening, or even later. Again, the point in time when a student's specific ability profile is described is likely to influence expectations concerning school performance.

For example, if a student is identified at the kindergarten screening as needing language intervention services, that may be the first time that the student and his family has been told about possible differences in that student's learning and development pattern. If the family went to the screening believing that the student was completely ready for kindergarten and having no ability differences, then this news is going to be shocking. How school personnel share information about students' ability profiles is important. If a family's first encounter with the school system includes information about how a child's abilities are lacking in some way, it is likely to influence how family members think about and react to later school encounters. In order to optimize the family–school relationship, school personnel must take into account the beliefs, perceptions, and experiences about a student's abilities prior to school entry (Boscardin, Brown-Chidsey, & Gonzalez-Martinez, 2002b).

Culture

A second important background feature for school personnel to take into account is the student's culture. The term *culture* is also generic; however, we have chosen to include it because it offers a way of understanding important aspects of students' life experiences outside of school. Students' cultural backgrounds can overlap with all the other experiences we discuss. However, culture patterns and beliefs are specific enough to warrant their own description. For example, students with hearing impairment or deafness have ability characteristics that must be taken into account by school personnel. They are likely also to have culture experiences that overlap with their ability profiles. In the United States there is an identifiable "deaf culture" that must be understood by educators. Within deaf culture, hearing is understood as anomalous and visual communication with ASL or SEE is the norm. Understanding the presence of deaf culture is critical for those who work with students who are deaf or hard-of-hearing.

There are numerous other cultures that educators also must understand. It would be impossible to list all of the cultural variations likely to influence school expectations. However, we will discuss some cultural patterns that may influence a student's school experiences. One important cultural pattern is expectations around family–school communication and interaction. For some culture groups, limited family–school communication is expected. In such cases, family members—as well as the student—expect that family events and school activities are entirely different and will not overlap. Similarly, some cultural traditions include specific ways of communicating with and referring to school personnel. For some cultures, very formal interactions are the norm. For example, the school principal, teacher(s), and other school personnel should always be referred to by their formal title, such as Dr., Ms., or Mr. In some cultures this expectation is reciprocal, and the parents and other family members expect to be called by their formal names too. If a teacher were to misunderstand this cultural expectation and refer to a parent or other family member by a first name, a significant miscommunication could occur (Boscardin, Brown-Chidsey, & Gonzalez-Martinez, 2002b). In other cultures, use of first names, even between children and parents or teachers, is accepted. All school personnel need to be aware of such cultural variations (Ortiz & Flanagan, 2002).

Language

As seen in the preceding examples, language is closely related to culture. Language and culture are interconnected and have a huge impact on students' school experiences (R. Lopez, 1997; Wright, 2004). There are differences of opinion regarding public school policies about language instruction. Some policymakers have advocated for English-only school instruction (Purdum, 1998). Others have supported full bilingual instruction that helps students maintain and strengthen their primary language while learning English (Cummins, 1986, 1996). Research findings have supported full bilingual instruction as the best choice for students' long-term educational outcomes (Willig, 1985). Regardless of the instructional policy and program(s) provided in school, educators must be aware of the effect that language proficiency has on school outcomes (E. Lopez, 1997). Students who are still learning English in an English-only school will be at a disadvantage compared to those who are fluent in English (August & Hakuta, 1997). The same is true for the parents and other family members. If a parent knows little or no English and that is the only language in which school documents are distributed, the parent will have great difficulty participating fully in his or her child's school experience. Similarly, it will be very difficult to have parents participate in the RTI process if the materials and communication are not provided in a common language.

Sometimes it is difficult to identify a student's or parent's English proficiency from observation alone. This is due to differences between two identified levels of language development: BICS and CALP (Cummins, 1979). BICS stands for Basic Interpersonal Communication Skills. CALP stands for cognitive academic language proficiency. BICS develop more quickly than CALP. Learners can develop BICS in English in about 2 years but need at least 5 years to develop CALP (Cummins, 1979). On the basis of observations with peers it may appear that a student or parent can communicate effectively in English (Boscardin, Brown-Chidsey, & Gonzalez-Martinez, 2002a). Oral communications with peers in a second language develop more rapidly than formal written language. Watching students and adults talk with others in English about everyday topics could provide a false impression of overall English language development. Nonverbal communication, including gestures and eye gaze, support such use of English by those still learning it. But conversational English is not the same as formal English usage. The ability to talk briefly with classmates and teachers is not the same as reading and writing English. For this reason, educators must not assume that a student or parent is fluent in English on the basis of brief verbal interactions alone. Instead, it is imperative that all those who work in schools be aware of the stages of English language acquisition and provide appropriate supports to those students and their family members who are still learning English.

Race

The United States has a complex racial history. Although recent decades have witnessed policies and practices designed to improve equal treatment of all persons under the law, a long legacy of racial discrimination and segregation cannot be erased overnight. Although all persons have nominal equality according to the U.S. Constitution and its amendments, ongoing evidence of racial inequality still exits. Regarding education, data continue to show that students of color, including African Americans, Hispanics, and Asians, have different educational outcomes than other students, especially Caucasians (National Center for Education Statistics, 2004). Despite evidence that students of all racial backgrounds share similar potential for school success (Helms, 1992), students from certain racial minorities often score lower on school assessment measures. Other evidence has shown that when students from racial minorities are provided with a combination of adequate resources and effective instruction, they perform as well as or better than racial majority students (Chall, 2000). As noted by Carter, Helms, and Juby (2004) and Tatum (1997), racial identity is a powerful factor in individual life experiences, including school. Importantly, racial identity affects all persons, regardless of skin color, and educators need to be aware of how race and racial identity influence students' school experiences.

Some of the seminal work on racial identity was conducted by Kenneth and Mamie Clark (Klein, 2004). This work showed the effects of negative racial identity and was used in the landmark 1954 *Brown v. Board of Education* U.S. Supreme Court case. That case brought attention to the differences in educational outcomes between students of color (primarily African Americans) and Caucasian students. The Brown decision declared that separate but "equal" schools were not allowable because the schools for African American students were substantially inferior to schools for Caucasian children. Despite many years of efforts to improve educational outcomes for students of color, there remains a racial divide in educational attainment (Carter et al., 2004). Specifically, students of color are less likely that Caucasians students to complete high school and be competitive wage earners (National Center for Education Statistics, 2004).

Knowledge about racial inequality in U.S. schools is important for those who implement RTI policies, because many of the students most in need of effective teaching and Tier 2 interventions are students from racial minorities. Being aware of how a student's racial identity had informed his or her mindset about school and personal goals is important. If a student, of any race, has decided that he or she cannot "do" the work expected in school, an additional hurdle on the path to school success is presented. In cases of low self-efficacy among students, educators need to know about and use instructional methods that include frequent reinforcers for attainment of specific goals. Additionally, educators need to be knowledgeable about the history of racial discrimination in the United States and be willing to confront racism when it is observed in schools. Equally important is equitable and representative coverage of the historical events important to the racial groups in each school setting.

Religion

Religion and religious practice have played a critical role in the history of the United States. All Native American cultures have strong religious traditions that are interwoven into their everyday practices. Similarly, European settlers in North America brought with them specific religious beliefs that defined their communities from the first days of settlement. While some early explorers and settlers traveled primarily for commercial reasons, others such as the Pilgrims and Puritans, as well as the Roman Catholic founders of

Maryland and the Spanish explorers in the coastal Pacific areas, brought with them various Christian traditions that have shaped North American values ever since. Indeed, those who wrote the first 10 amendments to the U.S. Constitution were so concerned about the freedom to practice one's own religious beliefs that such a protection was included in the First Amendment.

Despite constitutional protection of religious practice, schools have not been immune to conflicts and misunderstandings among students and staff of various faiths. Ranging from such matters as which holidays to include in school vacations to whether Christmas carols can be sung by school choirs, there are many ways in which religious beliefs and practices have an effect on school practices. Students who are absent from school due to religious celebrations may miss out on important events or be viewed by classmates as "outsiders." Specific religious doctrines also have been a source of dispute in schools. For example, in some communities there is widespread support for teaching a "creationist" view of human origins, while textbooks and science teachers generally subscribe to evolutionary principles. Although such issues are normally handled by the courts, there is apt to be a lingering effect from the public debate after the case is settled. For these reasons, educators need to be aware of the ways in which religious beliefs are a universal and significant human tradition.

FAIRNESS AND EQUITY IN EDUCATION

Related to all of the many ways that "diversity" can be interpreted is the issue of equity. As much as an appreciation for and celebration of all backgrounds and cultures may be a desirable goal, public schools have a specific defined task before them. That task is to provide an equitable education for all students who enroll. For this reason, it is imperative that all educators know about and be prepared to work with a wide variety of students, regardless of ability, culture, language, race, or religion. Given the highly mobile and international mixture of students enrolled in U.S. schools in the 21st century, it would be impossible for every teacher to be versed in all aspects of his or her students' backgrounds. Still, educators can be aware of their own expertise and limitations. Some teachers will be able to offer specialized skills such as bilingual instruction, special education, and knowledge about specific cultures. A critical element of what educators know and do to help students from diverse backgrounds relates to assessment practices.

Assessment

High-quality, reliable, and valid assessments are a cornerstone of RTI practices. Without accurate baseline data, it is impossible to know whether a student has made progress as a result of an intervention (Shinn, Collins, & Gallagher, 1998). *Accuracy* is the key to valid assessment. The extent to which assessment methods designed for majority group students will work with students from diverse backgrounds varies considerably (Boscardin, Brown-Chidsey, & Gonzalez-Martinez, 2002a). For example, a student who was born in the United States and grew up speaking, reading, and writing both Spanish and English equally may be able to take tests designed for the primarily English-speaking U.S. student majority. By contrast, a student who immigrated from another country very recently and is still mastering a BICS level of English proficiency should not be expected to participate in testing designed for students fluent in U.S. English and culture. For this reason, three major rules concerning assessment of students from diverse background should be followed during all RTI activities: (1) recognize that ability, culture, language, race, and/or religious variables may influence students' school performance; (2) evaluate a student's mastery of skills in the primary culture and language first; (3) plan and implement RTI activities that focus on attainment of instructional objectives while taking into account each student's unique background and characteristics.

Recognition of Diversity

The first step in conducting RTI practices that are fair and equitable is to identify the features present in students that are unique and diverse. This step seems very simple and yet may take considerable energy and planning. In order to know students' backgrounds, educators need to spend sufficient time with students and their families engaged in activities that enable families to share their experiences. School–community gatherings, family events at school, and informal contact between educators and family members all promote better understanding of the diversity present in the school population.

Background-Specific Assessments

In cases where a student's background is sufficiently unique that assessing using norm-referenced tests is not appropriate, alternative assessment procedures need to be used. A guiding principle for ascertaining whether a student should participate in a published norm-referenced assessment is to determine whether students with the same background were included in the norming sample (Salvia & Ysseldyke, 2004). If a student's background characteristics (e.g., language, race, culture, ability) were not represented in the norming sample, decisions about that student's educational performance should not be based on that test. For example, if students with Asperger's syndrome were not included in the norming sample for a given assessment, students with that disorder should not take the test. The same should hold true for students who are recent immigrants. This important principle creates a major challenge for educators whose job it is to teach all students, regardless of background. The best approach to take regarding assessment of students from diverse cultures is to start with an evaluation of each student's skill level mastery of instructional objectives. For example, if it is a stated instructional goal for all students in second grade to learn to subtract while borrowing from columns, then a baseline assessment of this skill is appropriate.

In the case of specific assessments, language diversity takes on a prominent role. Even when evaluating a student's math skills, a decision about what language to use in order to conduct the assessment must be made. In general, it is best to identify the student's dominant language as a first step toward RTI instructional planning. Language learning is a universal aspect of human development. Even among those with hearing and vision impairment, development of functional communication is a primary goal from the time of diagnosis. Once a student's primary language is identified, a decision about which language to use for subsequent instruction must be made. As noted earlier in this chapter, some school districts and states have adopted policies concerning English-only instruction that educators will need to observe. Ideally, students should be allowed to have formal instruction in multiple languages if that is observed to be a culturally or religiously valued goal. However, not all instruction must happen in school, and some language instruction (e.g., in Hebrew or Arabic) may have to occur outside the school setting. In situations where a student's family is fully bilingual and bilingual instruction is both desired and available, this is the optimal solution (Willig, 1985).

In situations where instruction in one language only is permitted, or where there is a time limit for transitional bilingual instruction, RTI procedures and decision-making needs to take into account the level of the student's current language development, including an estimate of current English proficiency. In many cases such an assessment will require the skills of a bilingual assessment professional. Such individuals are in short supply and may be unavailable for certain regions and languages. When a bilingual assessor is unavailable, a translator may be used, but this shortcoming must be noted in all assessment reports and the limitations related to the use of translators described. At a minimum, RTI assessment methods should include an estimate of the student's current skills in the language in which instruction will be provided. This estimate must be taken into account during all RTI procedures. Additionally, progress toward language development goals should be included in all RTI goals and progress monitoring. Given that fluency in standard English is both an explicit and implicit goal in all U.S. educational standards, including English progress monitoring in RTI activities is most likely a good idea (Baker, Plasencia-Peinado, & Lezcano-Lytle, 1998).

Appropriate Goal Setting

A related outgrowth of language-specific RTI assessment is goal setting. All RTI procedures involve evaluating students' progress toward certain goals, or benchmarks, and adjusting instruction to foster the target skill. In some cases, the nature of a student's goals will vary according to that student's unique characteristics. This is most obvious in the case of students with known disabilities. Certain disorders and conditions are likely to influence expected learning outcomes, and a student's goals should reflect these expectations. This is also the case for students with other diverse backgrounds. For example, in some cultures there may be different expectations for boys and girls. Teachers need to be aware of how family expectations may influence students' school performance. Similarly, in some cultures, it may be the norm for multiple generations to participate in child rearing and education decisions. Knowing which family members to invite to meetings is essential.

How RTI Connects Diverse Backgrounds

RTI methods are dynamic and designed to be used in ways that match the needs of specific students and populations. The choice of what interventions to try at each stage is up to those individuals charged with curriculum decision making in the school or district.

The only "rule" that must be followed when selecting specific interventions is that they be research-based. Also central to RTI is trying interventions and using data to determine whether student outcomes are enhanced. There is nothing in RTI to require that it be bound by specific ability, culture, language, race, or religious ideologies. For this reason, interventions can be matched to students' backgrounds and experiences. In many ways RTI methods are preferable to older models for curriculum and instructional decision making that focused primarily on instructional content. RTI focuses on ensuring that *all* students—regardless of ability, culture, language, race, and/or religion—obtain an education. The specific goals and content of the education are up to the local and state policymakers who determine learning standards and goals. In cases where specific learning outcomes are considered to be inappropriate for a student, alternative learning goals need to be set, usually within the framework of special education.

RTI methods offer educators a systematic and data-driven way to identify whether any given student is meeting specific learning goals. For this reason, RTI can help educators to bridge their various diverse backgrounds by focusing on common goals. In order to create and implement common goals, there need to be planning and development steps based on the backgrounds and experiences of the students involved. The best people to include in such planning are not only teachers but also parents, other family members, and community representatives who are interested in educational planning and growth for all students. Although differences between the school personnel and community members may seem large at first, a commitment to common goals can reduce that divide and foster better outcomes for all students.

CONCLUSION

This chapter has provided information concerning the use of RTI methods with students of differing abilities, cultures, languages, races, and religions. U.S. schools are becoming more diverse, and all educators need to make themselves aware of the unique backgrounds and experiences among the students and families in their district. As schools seek to improve educational outcomes for all students, they must incorporate practices that recognize and value the abilities, cultures, languages, races, and religions that students bring with them to school. RTI procedures can enhance school outcomes for diverse student populations by focusing on educational goals that reflect community values as well as state or national standards.

9

Using RTI Procedures as Part of Special Education Eligibility Decision Making

STUDENTS WITH ACADEMIC DIFFICULTIES

Fletcher et al. (2002), D. Fuchs (2003), and Kovaleski (2003) have shown that RTI methods are accurate for identifying which students need and will benefit from special education. O'Connor (2003) and Tilly (2003) have provided data to show that RTI methods reduce the number of students receiving special education services while increasing the quality of educational outcomes for all students. These findings indicate that RTI is an effective tool for supporting students' educational needs both before and after special education placement. While ongoing research about RTI practices needs to be conducted, the extant information supports the 10-step RTI model presented in Chapter 7 (Form 7.1). This chapter will include case examples of students whose school needs were supported with the use of RTI practices. First, an example of a student whose needs were met without special education is presented. It is followed by three examples of students whose responses to intervention revealed ongoing needs best addressed with special education.

Reading Fundamentals: The Case of Jody

Jody is a second-grade student who has struggled to learn to read. He lives with both his parents and little sister in a northeastern town. When Jody was an infant and toddler he spent his days at home with his mom. At age 3 he enrolled in a private preschool that focused on allowing students to explore and learn from self-directed inquiry. Jody began kindergarten in the same town where he attended preschool. The kindergarten classes were half-day sessions, and his teacher reported that he made good progress but was very shy and quiet in group settings. During the summer between kindergarten and first grade, Jody's family moved to Iowa. Jody enrolled in first grade along with students who had previously attended the local district's full-day kindergarten program. The district used the DIBELS as a measure of all students' literacy development, and Jody participated in fall DIBELS benchmarks. Jody's scores on letter naming fluency (LNF), phoneme segmentation fluency (PSF), and nonsense word fluency (NWF) are shown in Table 9.1. These scores show that, when compared to other first graders, Jody's scores reflected considerable risk of his not learning how to read.

Due to the high risk that Jody's fall DIBELS scores revealed, he was immediately placed in a Title I funded Tier 2 RTI intervention. The intervention included use of the evidence-based reading instruction program *Early Reading Intervention* (ERI) by Kame'enui and Simmons (2002). Jody's progress in learning to read was monitored using the nonsense word fluency DIBELS measure. In addition, Jody participated in the winter and spring DIBELS benchmarking activities; his scores on these measures are also shown in Table 9.1. Jody's weekly progress monitoring scores on NWF are plotted in Figure 9.1. These data show that once he began participating in the ERI program (a small-group intervention with 3–4 students in a group) he began to develop the skill of decoding nonsense words. By the time of the winter benchmarks, he was in the emerging range on NWF and his phoneme segmentation skills were established. By the time of the spring benchmarks all of his reading skills were in the low-risk range, and he had become a reader.

This case example shows how a student who appears to be very much at risk for reading difficulties, when given high-quality, evidence-based instruction, can achieve reading milestones and become a successful student. Another way of looking at Jody's situation is to ask what would have happened had he not participated in the ERI program. Based on data from research studies, it is likely that he would have struggled to understand that English words have parts consisting of shapes (letters) and sounds (phonemes). It is quite possible that he would have continued to struggle until his school performance was so low that he would have been referred for special education and identified as a student with a learning disability (Spear-Swerling & Sternberg, 1996). Instead, Jody was provided with evidence-based instruction and learned to read so that he could participate in all aspects of future school-based instruction.

Reading Roadblocks: The Case of Lilly

Lilly is a fourth-grade student. Lilly's teacher identified her as being at risk in reading because her fall benchmark score on oral reading fluency was 34, well below her class-

TABLE 9.1. Jody's Benchmark DIBELS Scores

Measure	Fall	Winter	Spring
Letter Naming Fluency	14	40	N/A
Phoneme Segmentation Fluency	9	11	36
Nonsense Word Fluency	3	29	48
Oral Reading Fluency	2	18	40

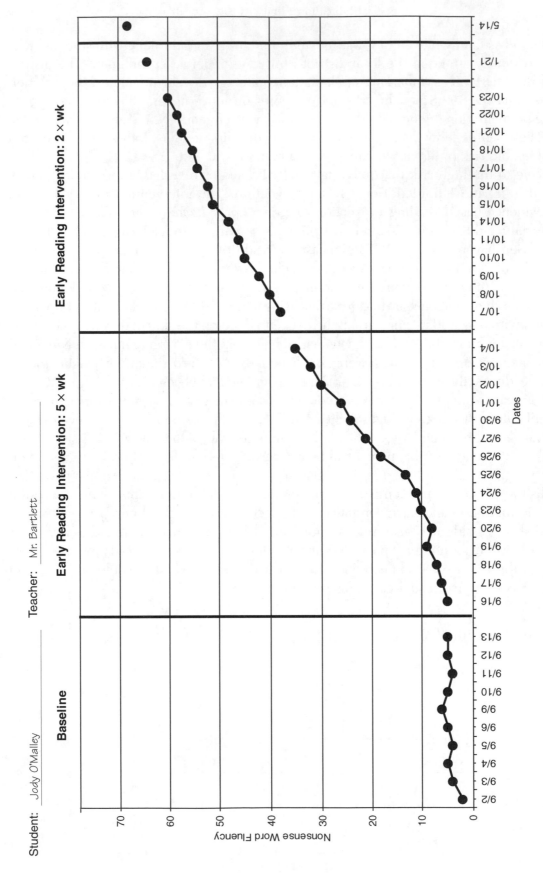

FIGURE 9.1. Jody's reading progress.

mates' scores and the national norm. Lilly's teacher decided to collect 2 weeks of oral reading fluency data before an intervention was tried because additional information about the stability and trend in Lilly's reading was desired. The baseline data confirmed that Lilly was able to read connected text, but only very slowly. In such cases, teaching students to read more rapidly helps them to develop fluency. Fluency is important because it involves both speed and accuracy. In the case of reading, fluency makes it possible for the reader to recognize and retrieve the shape and meaning of words so fast that other mental energy can be used for comprehension and reflection.

Lilly's baseline reading scores are shown in Figure 9.2. Since it appeared that Lilly needed to improve fluency, a scientifically based reading fluency intervention method known as repeated reading was implemented for 3 weeks. Repeated reading involves having the student reread passages both silently and orally multiple times to increase reading speed. At the end of 3 weeks the data were reviewed, and they revealed that Lilly made only modest gains, then plateaued. These data suggested that repeated reading was not effective in improving the student's reading fluency. For this reason another reading fluency intervention was used. Shadow reading involves having a student read orally at the same time as a teacher (or other "expert" reader). The mechanism at place in shadow reading is a reading model for the student to mimic. The expert reader shows the student what good, fast, and accurate reading sounds like. Additionally, the student gets multiple opportunities to practice reading because he or she reads along with the expert. This method has the benefit of making fluent reading explicit to the reader.

The shadow reading intervention was used with Lilly for 3 weeks and then the data were reviewed again. The graph revealed that the shadow reading method yielded only minimal increases in Lilly's reading fluency when compared with the previous intervention. Lilly's fluency remained in the 40s, well below the winter benchmark of 72 words per minute for fourth-grade students. Given that the teacher had tried two interventions and neither had resulted in the desired goal of increasing Lilly's reading fluency, a referral for special education was made. Of note, students with certain reading disabilities are characterized by very slow and labored reading, just as in the dysfluent reading seen in Lilly. Torgeson (2003) found that, even when these readers are given intensive scientifically based reading instruction, their reading fluency never becomes as strong as nondisabled readers. For this reason, it makes sense for Lilly to undergo a comprehensive evaluation for a reading disability. Such an evaluation would be likely to include measures of phonological awareness, rapid automatic naming (RAN), memory, and comprehension. Together, these data can be used to indicate whether Lilly has a reading disability. If she were to score below-average on measures of RAN as well as other indicators of memory, it would support the hypothesis that she has a specific learning disability in the area of reading.

Math Disdain or Disability: The Case of Rowena

Rowena is in the second grade and often expresses her dislike of math. Each day during math time she sighs and complains how hard the math problems are. On the fall math benchmarks Rowena scored 3 correct digits; the second-grade fall benchmark in math is

Student: Lilly Plummer   Teacher: Mrs. Brown

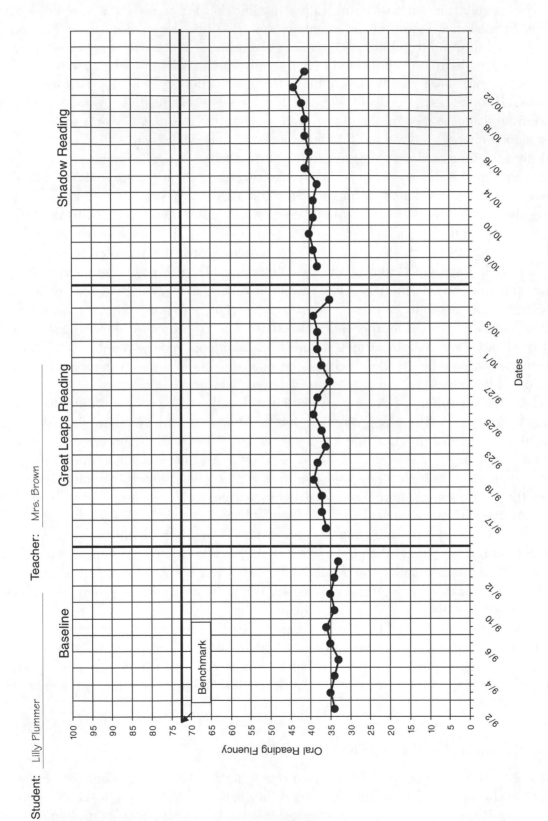

FIGURE 9.2. Lilly's reading progress.

112

17 correct digits. The benchmark items for second grade include addition problems of two one-digit numbers adding up to no more than 18. Because it appeared that Rowena knew at least some of her addition facts to 18, Rowena's teacher placed her in a math group of students who had all scored between 1 and 5 correct digits. Those students who had scored 0 were in another group because they did not appear to know *any* addition facts. Rowena's group of five students worked with the teacher for 15 minutes each day learning and practicing addition facts to 18. Each day, the students learned one new addition fact, practiced it in multiple formats (vertically, horizontally, and with a missing addend), and reviewed all previously learned facts on flash cards. After the 15-minute session with the teacher, the students completed a Great Leaps math sheet independently. The students' scores on the daily practice items were recorded and graphed, with the number of correct digits plotted (see Figure 9.3).

At the end of 3 weeks of small-group sessions, Rowena and her teacher reviewed her progress. Rowena had improved her digits correct score slightly; however, it improved only to a maximum of 6, still well below the fall benchmark. Due to Rowena's limited progress, her teacher placed her in a new math group. This group used the math instruction program known as *Touch Math*. As reviewed in Chapter 7 (Figure 7.6), Touch Math is a scientifically validated systematic and explicit instructional program to teach students computation skills and fluency. Touch Math lessons involve learning specific multisensory procedures for writing numerals and doing the four basic arithmetic operations. In Rowena's group, the teacher taught the students to write each of the students to write all nine numerals in the Touch Math format and then taught them how to add numbers to compute all sums up to 18. At the end of each Touch Math lesson, Rowena completed an addition problem assessment. On these assessments, Rowena improved to 9 digits correct in 1 minute; however, this was still quite a bit slower than the benchmark for students in her grade. Based on data from two separate math interventions for Rowena, her teacher decided to refer her for special education. Like Lilly, Rowena's math difficulty may involve memory and number retrieval. Those students who have difficulty holding information in memory while using it (working memory) sometimes struggle with arithmetic and other math skills.

Writing Blues: The Case of Maureen

Maureen is a fifth-grade student who detests writing. Her English teacher assigns daily writing tasks, and Maureen has yet to turn in any of these. At the beginning of the school year, all students in Maureen's fifth-grade completed CBM writing probes. These probes included "story starters" that the students completed by writing brief stories during 3-minute timed sessions. The benchmark number of words written in 3 minutes by fifth graders in Maureen's district is 70. Maureen scored a 0 on her fall writing benchmark because she did not write anything during the CBM sessions. As a result of concerns about Maureen's limited written production, her teacher spent time talking with her about writing and learned that Maureen had always disliked it. Maureen reported that in elementary school her teachers allowed her to submit alternative products in place of written work. For example, she was allowed to complete pictures, computer files with

Student: _Rowena Smedley_   Teacher: _Mrs. Bassingthwaite_

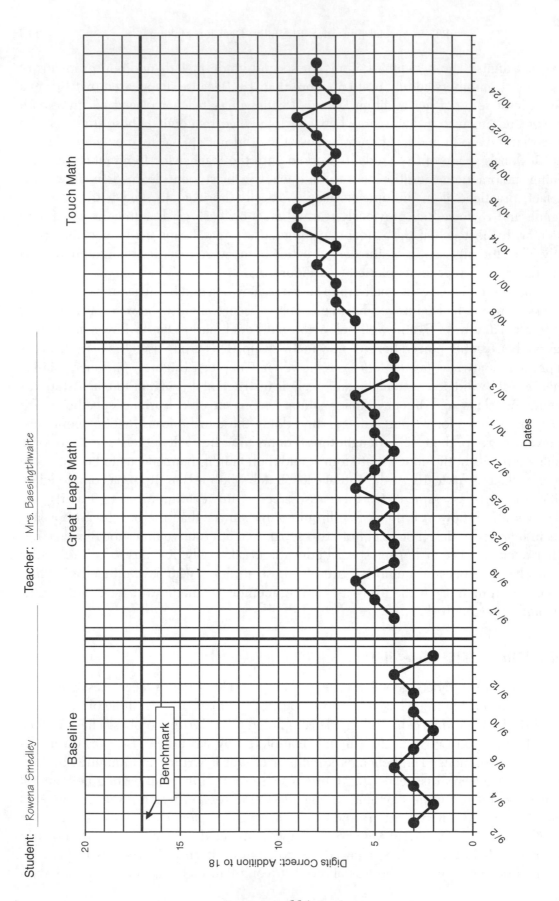

FIGURE 9.3. Rowena's math progress.

drawings, and oral reports instead of writing-based answers. When asked if she wanted to improve her writing skills, Maureen told her teacher that she could write a few words such as her name, telephone numbers, and other basics. Her teacher asked Maureen why she did not do any writing when it was assigned in school. Maureen replied that she did not see the point of writing because she could communicate in so many other ways.

After meeting with Maureen individually, her teacher reviewed Maureen's cumulative school record to learn if prior evaluation had been conducted. The file included an occupational therapy report completed when Maureen was in first grade. This report indicated that Maureen did not have any fine or gross motor problems that would interfere with writing tasks. Teacher reports covering Maureen's elementary school performance indicated that she had struggled or "refused" to complete writing tasks on a consistent basis for many years. Several teachers indicated that Maureen's writing problem was related to her "attitude" and that if she put her mind to it she would be able to produce grade-level-appropriate writing. Based on the information in the file and from her interview with Maureen, her teacher decided to use a writing intervention program titled Writing Skills with Maureen and two other students in her class.

First, the teacher collected additional baseline data from the students by having them complete CBM writing probes over a period of days. Once a stable trend in the students' writing scores was seen, the teacher began small-group writing lessons. The small-group lessons were held every day for 20 minutes. In order to assess students' progress, weekly CBM writing probes were administered. A summary of Maureen's baseline scores and performance on the weekly CBM probes is found in Figure 9.4. These data show that Maureen wrote a few more words after implementation of the small-group lessons, but the most words written over many weeks was 6. The other students in the writing group made much greater progress than Maureen. The teacher decided to refer Maureen for a special education evaluation because, despite Maureen's having the physical and cognitive skills to do written work, she only wrote a few words under normal conditions. And, despite highly specific and explicit writing instruction, Maureen's writing skills were not improving.

SUMMARY

The four case examples presented in this chapter demonstrate how RTI procedures can be used as part of a larger problem solving-based series of procedures to help students succeed in school. In the first case, Jody, the RTI activities resulted in the desired goal of having Jody learn to decode words. In the three other cases the RTI procedures did not result in the desired student goal, and the students were referred for comprehensive evaluations for special education. In Chapter 10, we extend the special education evaluation process to show how RTI data can be used as part of special education report writing and decision making.

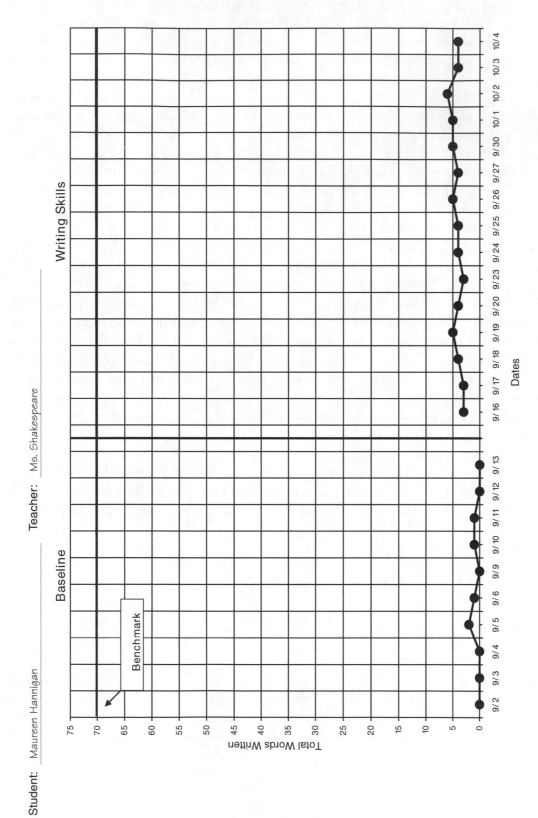

FIGURE 9.4. Maureen's writing progress.

116

10

RTI Reports

Formal Evidence of Student Progress

Reporting the data collected as part of RTI procedures is a critical step in the overall process. Chapters 7 and 9 include examples of some of the reporting formats and forms that can be used for communicating the results of RTI activities. This chapter will include a brief summary of all the different RTI forms and reports as well as a description of full-length evaluation reports based on RTI data. The chapter will conclude with three examples of RTI-based reports.

TYPES OF REPORTS

There are three main types of reports that could be generated from RTI data. These are brief summary reports, longitudinal data summary reports, and full psychological evaluation reports. We will discuss each in turn.

Brief Summary Reports

Brief summary reports are those used to communicate the status of a student's school progress at a given point in time. These can be created and used at a number of different times during the school year. The first ideal time for brief summary reports is in the fall after benchmark data have been collected. The brief summary report involves stating each student's performance on the benchmark measures and comparing that performance to local and/or national norms. Such brief reports provide an indicator of a student's relative progress and standing in the general curriculum. This same format can be repeated at each of the three benchmark data collection time points (October, January, May). Two sample benchmark brief summary reports are shown in Figure 10.1. The first

117

Student: Mark White					Teacher: Mary Brown			
Benchmark Date: September 25, 2004					Grade: 1			
	Student Score(s)			Local Norms*			National Norms**		
	Reading	Addition	Patterns	Reading	Addition	Patterns	Reading	Addition	Patterns
Fall	14	5	6	2–17	2–8	3–7	2–16	N/A***	N/A
Winter				13–46	5–11	6–9	12–42	N/A	N/A
Spring				31–87	9–15	7–9	26–75	N/A	N/A

*Local norms reflect the average range of scores obtained by all students who took the test.
**National norms reflect the average range of scores obtained by students from throughout the United States.
***National norms are not yet available for addition and patterns tasks.

Notes: Mark is off to a great start in reading and math. His scores indicate that he has the prerequisite skills to do the first-grade reading and math work we will cover this year.

If you have questions concerning this report, please contact your child's teacher.

Student: Mark White					Teacher: Mary Brown			
Benchmark Date: February 1, 2005					Grade: 1			
	Student Score(s)			Local Norms*			National Norms**		
	Reading	Addition	Patterns	Reading	Addition	Patterns	Reading	Addition	Patterns
Fall	14	5	6	2–17	2–8	3–7	2–16	N/A***	N/A
Winter	23	9	8	13–46	5–11	6–9	12–42	N/A	N/A
Spring				31–87	9–15	7–9	26–75	N/A	N/A

*Local norms reflect the average range of scores obtained by all students who took the test.
**National norms reflect the average range of scores obtained by students throughout the United States.
***National norms are not yet available for addition and patterns tasks.

Notes: Mark continues to make good progress in reading and math. His CBM scores reflect that he is learning the knowledge and skills we are covering. He is on track to meet the end-of-year grade-1 expectations.

If you have questions concerning this report, please contact your child's teacher.

FIGURE 10.1. Sample benchmark brief summary RTI reports.

report in Figure 10.1 shows Mark's fall CBM benchmark scores as well as the local and national norms. This brief summary indicates that Mark is off to a good start and should be able to handle the general education instruction planned for the year.

The second brief report shown in Figure 10.1 is the winter benchmark report. In this report both Mark's fall and winter benchmark data are included so that his parents can see the improvement he has made and how it compares with both local and national norms. The report includes space for a brief teacher summary note telling the parents what general conclusions can be drawn from the data presented. Some parents, or other report readers, may need help in understanding a report like this one the first time it is sent home. With help from teachers and other school personnel, parents can learn to interpret the brief report. Teachers may want to distribute such a report at regular parent–teacher conferences so that explanations about the report can be provided and any parent questions answered. The AIMSweb data management service includes parent reports as part of the many communication tools it offers (Edformation, 2004). These reports can be printed and mailed to parents or read by parents online.

Longitudinal Data Summary Reports

The second type of RTI report is a longitudinal data summary. This "report" is best made with the use of graphs such as those we have included throughout this book. These graphs tell the story of a student's progress once a specific intervention has been implemented. In addition to the graph, forms such as the Student Progress Review and the Referral for Special Education Worksheets found in Forms 7.9 and 7.11 (respectively) of Chapter 7 provide narrative summaries of student progress. These forms are specifically designed for teachers and other education personnel to use in determining the effectiveness of specific interventions for specific students. These worksheets probably are not sent home to parents but, rather, serve as the starting point for discussions, meetings, and decisions about student progress. For example, Figures 10.2 through 10.4 provide examples of a student's graphs and worksheets used to summarize his or her long-term progress toward specific goals.

In these figures, data for Guy Wyre are summarized. Guy is a third grader who is currently receiving instruction in a three-student group with Florence McPhee. Ms. McPhee is using the Phonographix reading instruction program. Guy was initially identified as needing additional reading instruction when he moved into the district during the spring of his second-grade year. He participated in the spring reading benchmarks and scored below the 10th percentile, as compared with other students in his new district. A Tier 2 small-group instruction program for Guy was implemented during the last few weeks of second grade, and it was resumed when he began the third grade. Guy's progress in the program has been monitored using the DIBELS Oral Reading Fluency (DORF) measure. As shown in Figure 10.2, Guy obtained scores of 15, 16, and 15 words read correctly during the fall benchmark and follow-up baseline testing in September 2004.

Guy's progress toward improved reading skills has been limited. His reading fluency increased from 15 words at the last baseline measure to 26 words at the 3-week review of his progress on October 4th. Because 26 words correct is just inside the national norm of 24–73 words per minute and Guy was making progress, it was decided to have Guy remain in the Phonographix program for at least another 3 weeks. The same decision was made on October 25th and November 16th. At each of these points in time, Guy's data indicated that he was making progress toward the reading benchmark. The Student Progress Review Worksheet for October 25th is shown in Figure 10.3. Decision points are marked with triangles on the graph in Figure 10.2. On December 7th Guy's progress was reviewed again. At this review, a different decision was made because his scores reflected very little growth during the preceding 3 weeks. Due to Guy's drop in reading progress, as well as a concern that he would not meet the winter benchmark goal, his small-group teacher referred Guy for a special education evaluation. The completed referral form is shown in Figure 10.4. Guy remained in the small-group instruction, pending a comprehensive evaluation.

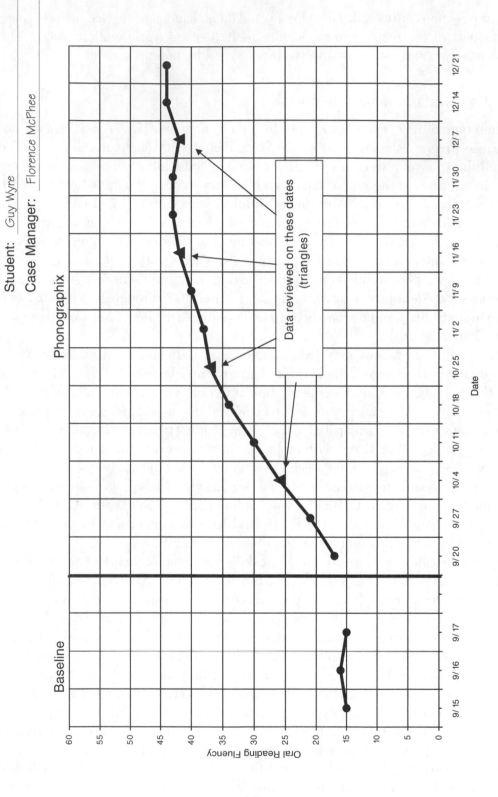

Student: _Guy Wyre_

Case Manager: _Florence McPhee_

FIGURE 10.2. Example of a completed Progress Monitoring Graph.

120

Student: Guy Wyre   Grade: 3   Teacher: Alice Green

Name of Tier 2 instruction program: Phonographix

Who is the teacher? Florence McPhee

How many students (total) are in the instruction group? 3

How often are the instructional sessions held? Daily

How long is each session? 40 minutes

How many sessions has this student attended? 63/65

Based on the progress-monitoring data, how many data points indicate that the student's skills are improving? 6
DECISION RULE: IF THE STUDENT HAS 3 OR MORE DATA POINTS SHOWING IMPROVEMENT, MAINTAIN THE PROGRAM

Based on the progress-monitoring data, how many data points indicate that the student's skills are not improving? 0
DECISION RULE: IF THE STUDENT HAS 3 OR MORE DATA POINTS SHOWING NO IMPROVEMENT, CHANGE THE PROGRAM

How do the student's current skills compare to typically achieving peers? Guy's current score of 37 is within the minimum benchmark of 23 for beginning-of-the-year grade-2 students, but below the winter benchmark of 40 words.
DECISION RULE: IF THE STUDENT HAS 6 OR MORE DATA POINTS SHOWING PERFORMANCE AT GRADE LEVEL, DISCONTINUE

Based on the obtained data, what modifications to the current instructional program will be made? No modifications will be made. Guy continues to make progress in reading.

When will the modifications go into effect? N/A

When will the student's progress be reviewed again? Monday, November 16

ALL PROGRESS-MONITORING DATA AND GRAPHS REFERENCED ABOVE MUST BE ATTACHED

Person completing this form: Florence McPhee, MEd   Date: October 25, 2004

FIGURE 10.3. Example of a completed Student Progress Review Worksheet.

Student _Guy Wyre_   **Grade** 3   **Teacher** _Florence McPhee_

Describe how student's instructional need was initially identified:

Guy scored in the at-risk range on the 2nd-grade DIBELS at the spring benchmark period last year. This fall, Guy scored in the at-risk range on the fall 3rd-grade reading benchmarks.

Tier 2 instructional methods that were used to improve student's knowledge/skills:

Small-group Phonographix lessons with three students in the group were begun the week beginning September 20. Guy's progress was monitored using weekly oral reading fluency probes. Guy made progress in reading for 6 weeks; however, his progress slowed after December 7 and indicates that he is no longer making progress toward better reading skills.

Who provided the Tier 2 instructional program?

Florence McPhee, certified highly qualified special education teacher

Progress-monitoring measure used to record student's progress during Tier 2 instruction:

Oral reading fluency probes

Tier 2 program start date _September 20, 2004_ **Tier 2 program review date(s)** _October 4, 25, November 16, 2004_

Describe the student's current instructional need(s):

Guy needs to learn more words and read text more quickly.

What, if any, additional instruction or supports is this student currently receiving?

Guy is receiving 40 minutes per day of Phonographix 3:1 instruction until a comprehensive evaluation can be completed.

ALL PROGRESS-MONITORING DATA AND GRAPHS REFERENCED ABOVE MUST BE ATTACHED

Person completing this form: _Florence McPhee, MEd_   **Date:** _December 7, 2004_

FIGURE 10.4. Example of a completed Tier 3 Referral for Special Education Worksheet.

Full Psychological Evaluation Reports

The third type of RTI report is a comprehensive psychological evaluation report. This report is very similar to other types of reports already used in schools. Such reports serve the purpose of describing and documenting a student's school progress and needs. RTI data can easily be integrated into such reports and offer an important source of information concerning what has already been implemented to assist a student. We will describe the components of full evaluation reports and then provide three examples of such reports.

EVALUATION REPORT COMPONENTS

The components of full evaluations using RTI data are the same as those found in solution-focused reports (Brown-Chidsey & Steege, 2005). A summary of the key elements in solution-focused RTI reports is presented in Table 10.1. There are three main sections in solution-focused reports: (1) problem identification, (2) problem definition, and (3) exploring solutions. These sections correspond to the first three stages of the problem-solving model described in Chapter 1. RTI data can be used in each of these report sections.

Problem Identification

Problem identification is the first point at which the "problem" appears on the "radar screen." This section includes three major pieces of information: (1) student's name, age, grade, classroom, (2) date(s) when the problem was observed and a basic description of

---

TABLE 10.1. Solution-Focused Evaluation Report Outline

1. Identification of the problem
   a. Student's name, age, grade, classroom
   b. Date(s) when problem was observed
   c. Names and positions of those who identified the problem

2. Definition of the problem
   a. Background information about the student
   b. Current educational placement
   c. Present levels of performance
      • Student
      • Typically achieving peers
   d. Magnitude of difference between the student's performance and what is expected
   e. Summary of the problem definition

3. Possible solutions
   a. General education interventions
   b. Special education interventions

Note. From Brown-Chidsey and Steege (2005, p. 272). Copyright 2005 by The Guilford Press. Reprinted by permission.

the problem, and (3) the names and positions of those who identified the problem. The identifying information contained in items (1) and (3) is very straightforward. The student's name, age, grade, and current teacher should be listed. If the student has more than one main teacher who has participated in the RTI activities, all the participating teachers should be listed. Item (2) is the place where RTI information can be given. Here the details of the student's performance and the conditions under which the data were collected are provided. For example, this item could be filled in as follows:

> All third-grade students were administered CBM reading benchmarks during September 2004. Seth's score of 19 words per minute falls below the 10th percentile, indicating that his current reading skills are lower than 90% of his classmates.

The problem identification section of the report serves the purpose of orienting the reader to the subject and focus of the report and does not need to be long. The next section provides the details about how and why the student's situation is problematic.

Problem Definition

This section of the report contains the essential data concerning the overall circumstances surrounding a student's school performance. There are five elements in this section: (1) background information about the student, (2) the student's current educational placement, (3) the student's present levels of performance as well as information about the performance of typically achieving peers, (4) the magnitude (size) of the difference between the student's performance and what is expected, and (5) a summary of the problem definition.

Background Information

The background information section includes more detailed aspects of a student's experience than is covered in the identifying information in section 1. The background section tells the student's "story," from the earliest point of relevance to the current day. In many cases the background section begins with a summary of prenatal, perinatal, and neonatal health obtained from the mother or another family member. In the case of certain disabilities (e.g., cerebral palsy) the presence or absence of symptoms from birth is required for accurate diagnosis. In addition to pregnancy and birth information, a brief summary of any childhood illnesses or medical conditions should be provided. This is important because chronic medical conditions usually have an effect on school performance. Similarly, brief histories of the student's social and educational experiences should be included. The social history includes descriptions of the neighborhood(s), location(s), or setting(s) in which the child has been raised. Included here would be information about living on- or off-base if a family is in the military. Also appropriate here would be information about the family and home environment (e.g., siblings, stepparents, grandparents).

The educational history begins at whatever point the student entered out-of-home childcare. For some students, this will occur at the point of kindergarten entry. For those students who attended any kind of out-of-home childcare or preschool program, the basic information about those experiences should be included. After describing preschool experiences, the student's progress in school should be summarized. Even if a student made expected (typical) progress, that should be noted. For students who have previously been identified with a disability or who have repeated a grade or received other support services, specific mention of these experiences should be made. The educational history section should go up to the point in time just before the current educational placement.

Current Educational Placement

This item in the report is very brief and includes only one or two sentences describing the student's current classroom(s). If the student participates in multiple classrooms, all subjects and classes should be mentioned.

Present Levels of Performance

Once the current educational setting has been described, the report turns to a description of how well the student is doing in the current setting. This is another place in the report where RTI data should be included. In this part of the report, more extensive RTI data can be reported. Specifically, all the scores obtained by the student during RTI instruction should be summarized here. Since it is easiest to understand a student's progress when such data are summarized in a graph, the actual graph used to track the student during RTI activities should be attached to the report and referenced here. In addition, the report should include a narrative summary of the data, indicating under what instructional conditions the student did, or did not, make progress. If CBM survey-level assessment procedures were conducted in addition to the progress monitoring activities, those data should be reported in this section as well.

In many cases there will be more than just RTI or survey-level assessment data to include in the report. The RTI data should be described first and followed by other data or scores. For example, a student may have been given several standardized, norm-referenced tests as part of the evaluation procedures (Flanagan & Ortiz, 2001). Scores from tests such as the Comprehensive Test of Phonological Processing (CTOPP), Woodcock–Johnson Tests of Cognitive Abilities, Third Edition (WJ-III/COG), or the Children's Memory Scale (CMS) should be summarized and included in the report. For every standardized score reported, it is important that more than just the stand-alone score number be given. In addition to the standardized score, the report author should include the confidence interval, indicating the true range of scores as well as the percentile rank for the score. Authors are encouraged to omit reporting age- and grade-equivalent scores, as these are much less reliable than standard scores.

Magnitude of Difference(s)

Once the RTI data are summarized, the extent to which the student's scores differ from those of other students or from expected scores needs to be addressed. It is the magnitude, or size, of the difference between the student's obtained scores and expected or desired scores that really *defines* the problem. This is an important distinction, because the data may reflect a "problem," but one so small as to not merit a major initiative to fix it. Alternatively, the problem may be very large and require intensive and substantial resources to address. For example, a straight-A student who receives a B+ on one history test is not in danger of failing the class or dropping out of school. By contrast, a sixth-grade student who cannot read at all has a huge problem, because virtually all sixth-grade instruction requires reading skills. The large magnitude of that student's problem justifies an intensive remedy. It is important that report authors keep in mind that they are not supposed to determine if a student is eligible for special education. That decision is reserved for the special education team, including the student's parents. However, the report may describe the nature of the student's school needs in terms that match up with certain disability criteria if the data support such a description.

Report Summary

The final part of the problem definition section is a brief summary of the problem definition. This represents the report author's best opportunity to state the nature of the student's school difficulties in clear, unambiguous language. This section should be concise and deliver a solid "take-home" message about the student's needs. For example, the summary could state:

> Martha is a 10-year-old student who is experiencing difficulty with math assignments. Data from RTI procedures revealed that Martha made limited gains in math computation proficiency when provided with small-group intensive computation instruction. Follow-up testing revealed below-average scores on measures of rapid automatic naming (RAN), short-term memory, and general math achievement. Additional testing showed that she has strong general problem-solving and verbal skills. The data obtained as part of this evaluation suggest that Martha exhibits characteristics consistent with a learning disorder, math subtype.

Exploring Solutions

The last section of the report involves exploring solutions to the identified problem(s). This section may be divided into two subsections related to the type(s) of intervention(s) considered: general education or special education. While students who are being evaluated for a possible learning disability will have already participated in at least one or more general education intervention(s), it may be the case that the best possible solution for the student still lies in general education. For example, large school districts may offer a wide range of primary grades reading and math support funded by Title I. It may be that a student participated in one or more of these as part of RTI, but the ones used were not successful. If the evaluation data suggest that a student is likely to be successful in a different Title I program, that program should be tried, even if the student is identified as having a disability. Alternatively, if the best solution for a student's presenting problem appears to be a special education program, then those kinds of solutions should be considered. In writing the solutions section of the report, authors must keep in mind that they need to explain the type of instruction hypothesized to be helpful for a specific student.

Importantly, the proposed solutions are hypotheses that need to be tested. Until data are collected that verify the efficacy of any given program, it is only a hypothesis. Since data about a student's progress in any program will need to be collected, report authors should suggest ideal progress-monitoring instruments to match specific instruction. Having the progress-monitoring indicator already ready at the time an intervention begins makes it much easier to measure student progress from the first day of the intervention.

REPORT EXAMPLES

The last part of this chapter includes three report examples. The first report reflects a situation in which a student was not identified as a student with a disability. The second report shows a student who was identified as having a disability and was subsequently provided with special education services. The last report shows how some evaluations are inconclusive and lead to additional assessment. The "students" in the reports are fictitious but based on characteristics and data from real students we have evaluated. In each case, the student participated in RTI procedures prior to referral for evaluation.

Mary Ann's Math Troubles: No Disability Found

In the first report, we show how RTI data were used as a starting point to determine whether a student was eligible for special education services. This report summarizes information about Mary Ann, a third-grade student with poor math performance. Mary Ann's score on the fall CBM math benchmark was very low; she completed only 3 digits correctly on the mixed addition and subtraction probes. In comparison, the average score for all third graders in Mary Ann's district was 11 digits correct. Because her teacher was concerned about Mary Ann's performance, she implemented small-group math instruction for Mary Ann and two classmates with similarly low scores on the fall testing. These small-group lessons were held in the classroom every weekday morning for 20 minutes. The lessons included direct instruction of specific addition facts, practice of the facts learned to date, and a math facts "game" that featured rapid retrieval of addition facts as the key to winning. Student progress toward benchmark addition skills was monitored with weekly CBM addition probes. Mary Ann's scores on the weekly probes are shown in Figure 10.5. As the graph shows, Mary Ann made limited progress on learning math facts over 3 weeks of the small-group lessons.

Because the other students in Mary Ann's group were ready to move on to subtraction lessons and she was not, her teacher decided to work with Mary Ann and one other student using the Touch Math program. Again, weekly data were collected. Mary Ann's progress in Touch Math is recorded in the right-hand section of Figure 10.5. As with the earlier intervention, she made only limited progress. Mary Ann's teacher decided to refer Mary Ann for a comprehensive evaluation for special education. The following report integrates the data from Mary Ann's RTI sessions with subsequent additional assessment information.

Student: Mary Ann Hartwick   **Teacher:** Mrs. Morgan

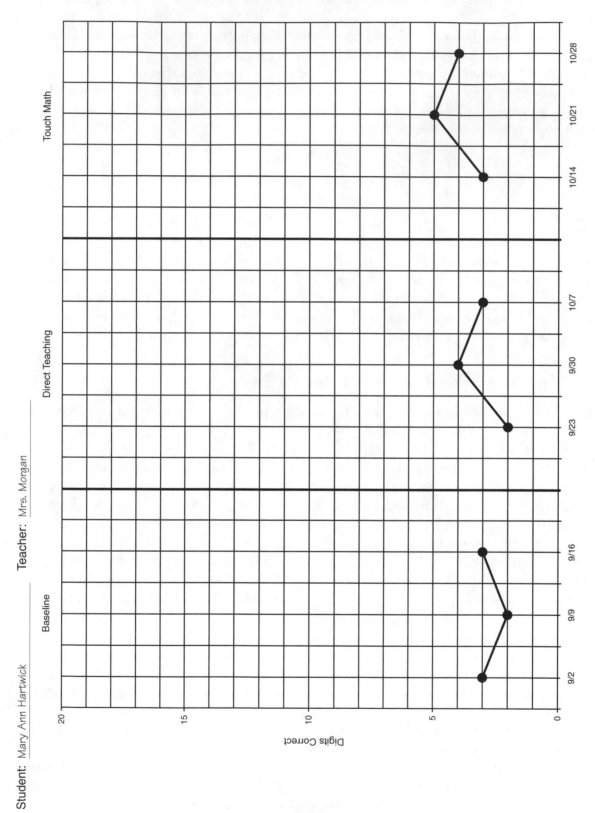

FIGURE 10.5. Mary Ann's math progress.

CONFIDENTIAL
Crabapple Cove School District
Seaside, Maine
Psychological Evaluation

Name: Mary Ann Hartwick   Grade: 3rd
Date of Birth: 1/17/65   Evaluation Dates: 1/18, 1/20, and 1/25/05
Age: 9–0   Report Date: 11/15/05

IDENTIFICATION OF PROBLEM

On September 15, 2004, all third-grade students in Crabapple Cove School District were given curriculum-based measures of reading and math proficiency. Mary Ann scored above the target level for reading, but scored well below the target for math. Her teacher, Patricia Morgan, identified Mary Ann as a student needing additional math instruction and small-group math lessons, taught by Mrs. Morgan, were begun on September 23, 2004.

DEFINITION OF PROBLEM

Background Information about Student

Mary Ann has attended school in the Crabapple Cove District since kindergarten. An interview with her mother held on January 3, 2005, revealed that Mary Ann reportedly likes the social aspects of school but not the academic work. Mrs. Hartwick reported that Mary Ann was born without complications after a full-term pregnancy. Mary Ann has two younger siblings, Matt (age 6) and Cecily (age 3). Mrs. Hartwick explained that Cecily has cerebral palsy and receives in-home services for her needs under an Individualized Family Service Plan (IFSP). Mrs. Hartwick said that Mary Ann was very healthy as a baby and that her school absences were related to difficulties getting Mary Ann to school and frequent family trips to obtain medical services for Mary Ann's little sister.

Review of Mary Ann's school records showed that she met all milestones at the kindergarten screening and made good progress during her kindergarten year. No problems with overall skill development were noted. Teacher reports from first grade included frequent mention of Mary Ann being absent from school often. Correspondence between the school principal and Mary Ann's parents indicated that these absences were due to complications with Mrs. Hartwick's third pregnancy and the subsequent delivery of Cecily. Similar teacher reports and parent communications from second grade were also found in Mary Ann's file. Mary Ann's benchmark CBM scores from first grade and second grade show initial average performance followed by a decline in scores, starting in the middle of second grade. An interview with Mary Ann's second-grade teacher revealed that he was worried about Mary Ann's progress but decided to wait until third grade to do anything because Mary Ann was absent some part of every week during March, April, and May of the year.

Current Educational Placement

Mary Ann is currently enrolled in a general education third-grade class at Jenkins Elementary School in Seaside, Maine. Review of Mary Ann's first two report cards for the year showed that she is quiet and withdrawn on the days she is present, but that she was absent 36 out of 68 school days.

Sources of Information

Information concerning Mary Ann's present level of school performance was obtained from the following sources:

> Interviews with Mary Ann, Mrs. Hardwick, and Mary Ann's teachers
> Fall CBM benchmarks
> RTI (Tier 2) progress data
> Key Math Test
> Children's Memory Scale
> Rapid Naming subtests of the Comprehensive Test of Phonological Processing
> Achenbach System of Empirically Based Assessments

The scores obtained from these assessments are summarized in the accompanying tables [Tables 10.2–10.5].

The tables include information that can be used to compare Mary Ann's performance with that of other students her age. The CBM scores show that Mary Ann is reading better than many fourth-grade students, but her math performance is much weaker. Additional math assessment with the Key Math Test showed that Mary Ann's math skills are below-average in all areas. Both her Children's Memory Scale and Rapid Naming test scores are in the average range when compared with norms from a national sample of students her age. These scores suggest that Mary Ann has average memory and retrieval skills for a girl of her age.

Both Mary Ann's mom and teacher provided responses on the Achenbach Child Behavior Checklist indicating that Mary Ann often appears withdrawn and sad. These psychological evaluation data as well as interviews revealed that Mary Ann evidences characteristics associated with a depressed state. An interview with Mary Ann was consistent with the Achenbach scores. Mary Ann reported that she is sad "all the time" and "wished she could make her sister better." Mary Ann also reported that she likes it when she gets to stay home and help her mom because it makes her feel "useful." When asked if she thought that missing so much school might hurt her learning, Mary Ann responded by saying, "Yes, but what good is school anyway if the doctors can't make my sister better?"

Summary of Problem Definition

The combined evaluation information presented here suggests that Mary Ann's math skills are lower than expected for a third-grade student in Crabapple Cove School District. These apparent difficulties have been observed in classroom performance, CBM testing, and on a comprehensive math assessment. While there is a strong consistency in Mary Ann's math scores and performance, evaluation results from assessment of memory skills indicate that the subskills necessary for fluent

TABLE 10.2. Mary Ann's Curriculum-Based Measurement Scores and Local Benchmark Scores

Test	Mary Ann's score	Local benchmark range
Reading (oral reading fluency)	126	72–122
Math (addition and subtraction fluency)	3	11–15

TABLE 10.3. Mary Ann's Key Math Test Scores

Subtest	Standard score	Percentile rank	Confidence interval
Basic Concepts	81	9	75–87
Operations	78	3	73–83
Applications	73	2	66–80

TABLE 10.4. Mary Ann's Children's Memory Scale Scores

Subtest	Standard score	Percentile rank	Confidence interval
Immediate Verbal Memory	99	49	93–105
Delayed Verbal Memory	98	47	91–105
Immediate Visual Memory	101	51	96–106
Delayed Visual Memory	102	52	96–108
General Memory	100	50	95–105

TABLE 10.5. Mary Ann's Comprehensive Test of Phonological Processing Scores

Subtest	Scaled score[a]	Percentile rank	Confidence interval
Rapid Color Naming	9	48	6–12
Rapid Digit Naming	10	50	7–13
Rapid Letter Naming	11	52	8–14
Rapid Object Naming	12	55	9–15
Rapid Naming Quotient	101	56	95–107

[a] Scaled scores have a mean of 10 and standard deviation of 3; quotients have a mean of 100 and standard deviation of 15.

math computation appear to be intact. Specifically, no deficits or difficulties with rapid automatic naming or other memory skills were observed. The lack of any below-average scores on the memory tests suggests that Mary Ann's school difficulties are related to factors others than memory. Mary Ann did exhibit characteristics associated with a depressive disorder. Her own report, as well as those of her teacher and mother, indicated that she feels sad most of the time.

Taken all together, the evaluation results can be used to generate a hypothesis about Mary Ann's school difficulties. The data suggest that Mary Ann's math problems may be related to her poor school attendance and depressed state. The following suggestions for validating this hypothesis and solving the problem are offered for consideration.

POSSIBLE SOLUTIONS

The following recommendations are based on the current assessment data and are offered for consideration by the team:

1. Increase Mary Ann's attendance and participation in school activities, including math instruction.
2. Reinforce Mary Ann for accurate math work completion.
3. Help Mary Ann's family access family counseling to address the effects of her sister's medical status and needs on the family; Mary Ann may benefit from brief cognitive-behavioral therapy to promote better coping skills. The family may want to consider a referral for additional mental health services for Mary Ann.
4. Provide intensive remedial math instruction to bring Mary Ann's skills up to fourth-grade level.

John Q. Smith, EdS, NCSP
School Psychologist

Luke: Identification of Disability Using RTI and Cognitive Measures

Luke Walters is a second-grade student with math difficulties. The following sample report shows how RTI procedures were used to identify a learning disability. In Luke's case, RTI methods were used to improve his math skills. When these did not work, he was referred for an evaluation and found to have a specific math disorder.

CONFIDENTIAL
Sunnyside School District
Happy Valley, Oregon
Psychological Evaluation

Name: Luke Walters   Grade: 3rd
Date of Birth: 3/16/97   Evaluation Dates: 11/9, 11/12, and 11/14/04
Age: 8–10   Report Date: 12/01/04

IDENTIFICATION OF PROBLEM

In September 2004 Luke participated in fall curriculum-based measurement of all students' reading and math skills. While Luke's reading skills were observed to be in the average range, his math scores were well below the expected target for third-grade students.

DEFINITION OF PROBLEM

Background Information about Student

Luke has attended Sunnyside Elementary School since kindergarten. He has made suitable progress in most skills areas, but a review of his records indicates that he struggled with math in kindergarten and first grade. In kindergarten, Sunnyside students learn counting and quantity skills. By the end of kindergarten, students are expected to be able to count to 100. Luke was able to count only to 52 at the end of his kindergarten year. In first grade Luke again struggled with math and received Title I math instruction. He worked in a small group for 30 minutes each day throughout the year on learning to add single digits up to a sum of 10. By the end of first grade Luke obtained a score of 8 digits correct on the spring CBM benchmark. At the beginning of second grade Luke again displayed difficulty with math skills. On the fall math CBM benchmark Luke scored 3 digits correct. The district's CBM data indicated that students who scored below 17 correct digits were at risk for ongoing math difficulties.

Current Educational Placement

Due to his score on the fall benchmark, Luke was provided with daily small-group math instruction. This instruction included using the Great Leaps Math program to build students' fluency with basic computation skills. Progress-monitoring data collected during the intervention showed that Luke scored between 4 and 6 digits correct over 3 weeks of the Great Leaps intervention. Due to Luke's limited progress, a new intervention was tried. He moved into a group using the Touch Math program. This program includes direct and sequenced math skills instruction. Progress-monitoring data revealed that Luke gained only 2 points after using the Touch Math program for 3 weeks. At the end of October, Luke's teacher referred him for a comprehensive evaluation for special education.

Student: _Luke Walter_   Teacher: _Mrs. Tilton_

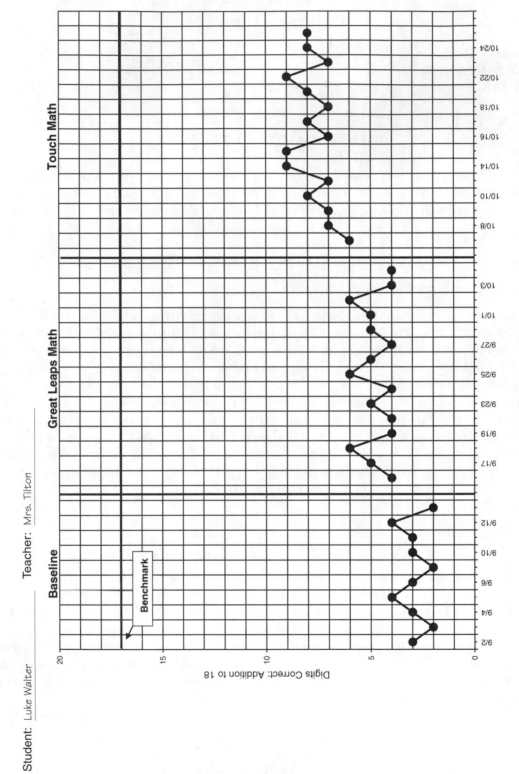

FIGURE 10.6. Luke's math progress.

134

Sources of Information

Information concerning Luke's present level of school performance was obtained from the following sources:

> Interviews with Luke, Mr. Walters, and Luke's teachers
> Fall CBM benchmarks
> RTI (Tier 2) progress data

The scores obtained from benchmark and Tier 2 assessments are summarized in the accompanying figure [Figure 10.6].

Summary of Problem Definition

Luke's current math computation skills are well below what is expected of grade 2 students at Sunnyside Elementary School. Two interventions designed to improve Luke's computation skills resulted in minimal progress. Given that Luke has made adequate progress in all school areas except math and that he did not respond to two scientifically based math instruction programs, it appears that his math difficulties can best be understood as a specific math learning disability.

POSSIBLE SOLUTIONS

The following recommendations are based on the current assessment data and are offered for consideration by the team:

1. Luke may benefit from more intensive math instruction. He may need individualized daily math instruction that focuses on mastering basic computation fluency.
2. Luke is likely to benefit from short-term counseling and instruction to understand what learning disabilities are and how they affect those who have them.

Mary Snell, PhD, NCSP
School Psychologist

Jane: Additional Assessment Is Needed

In the case of Jane, the data obtained from the evaluation were inconclusive. When the data obtained as part of an evaluation do not yield a clear answer, then additional assessment should be conducted. It is appropriate to summarize the initial data in a preliminary report so that all team members can be made aware of what evaluation procedures have been conducted as well as what additional assessments need to be conducted and when.

CONFIDENTIAL

Eastland River School District
Morrisville, Kansas
Psychological Evaluation

Name: Jane Murrey

Date of Birth: 7/11/94

Age: 10-4

Grade: 5th

Evaluation Dates: 11/2, 11/3, and 11/4/04

Report Date: 11/21/04

IDENTIFICATION OF PROBLEM

Jane was reported by her classroom teacher to have significant reading difficulties.

DEFINITION OF PROBLEM

Background Information about Student

Jane moved to Eastland in July 2004. Prior to living in Eastland, her family lived in several towns in central Kansas. No educational records from Jane's prior schools were found in her cumulative folder. Efforts to contact Jane's parents to obtain additional information about Jane's educational history were not successful. Jane scored 34 on the fall CBM reading assessment. The fall reading goal for fifth-grade students is 70 words per minute.

Current Educational Placement

Jane is currently enrolled in Nancy Adams's class at Eastland Elementary. Due to Jane's low scores on baseline reading assessment measures given in follow-up to the fall benchmark, her teacher implemented the Great Leaps reading program with Jane and several other students. Jane's progress in the Great Leaps program was monitored with oral reading fluency probes twice per week. These scores were graphed and revealed that Jane made no progress in her reading fluency. On October 8th Ms. Adams moved Jane to a new reading group that used the shadow reading procedure. This procedure involves having the students read along with and right after the teacher to improve reading fluency. Data collected twice a week during the shadow reading intervention revealed that Jane made limited progress.

Sources of Information

Information concerning Jane's present level of school performance was obtained from the following sources:

> Interview with Jane
> Fall CBM benchmarks
> RTI (Tier 2) progress data

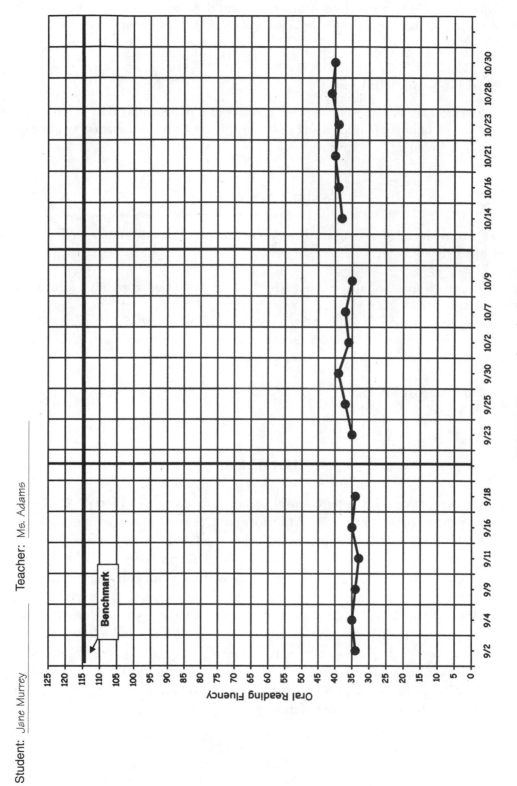

FIGURE 10.7. Jane's reading progress.

137

The scores obtained from benchmark and Tier 2 assessments are summarized in the accompanying figure [Figure 10.7]. In addition to the intervention data, in an interview with Jane she reported that she has always struggled with reading and that she would like to become a better reader. Jane reported that there are few books at home and that her parents work too late to read to her each night.

Summary of Problem Definition

Jane's current reading skills are well below what is expected of beginning fifth-grade students at Eastland. Efforts to improve Jane's reading skills using Great Leaps and shadow reading did not result in improved reading performance.

POSSIBLE SOLUTIONS

The following recommendations are based on the current assessment data and are offered for consideration by the team:

1. Additional information about Jane's school history is needed; ongoing efforts to contact her parents are suggested.
2. More specific information about Jane's reading skills is needed. Such information is usually obtained from individualized testing. Parental consent to conduct a detailed evaluation of Jane's reading skills is recommended.

Darcy McGuire, MS, NCSP
School Psychologist

SUMMARY

This chapter has provided a report template and examples of RTI reports. There are three main types of reports used with RTI procedures: brief summary reports, longitudinal data summary reports, and full psychological evaluation reports. Each of these reports provides information about the success of specific RTI procedures. Brief reports are designed to be used with all students to share information about general progress. Longitudinal reports provide information that can be used to determine whether an intervention is working. Evaluation reports are used as part of the special education referral process and incorporate RTI data from longitudinal reports but also include other assessment data. In order for RTI data to be maximally useful it must be communicated with those who can use it to make decisions about students' instructional needs. These report formats offer differentiated ways of sharing RTI data so that teachers, parents, and students can participate in educational planning.

11

Training Educators
to Use RTI Methods

TRAINING PROCEDURES

In order for RTI procedures to be effective for students, many educational personnel can—and should—participate in RTI activities. In order for accurate implementation to occur, teachers, paraprofessionals, specialists, and administrators will need to learn how to use RTI methods. This chapter includes information related to training teachers and others how to use RTI procedures.

A NEEDED PARADIGM SHIFT

One of the first and most critical parts of RTI training is to help all educators understand the underlying components included in RTI methods. For many, the core RTI model will be a significant paradigm shift. As noted in Chapter 1, traditional ways of seeing students' school needs have tended to focus on medically based disabilities in which the student is considered the problem. By contrast, RTI methods focus on a new problem definition in which the problem is measured by the distance between what is expected and what is occurring. Instead of the student being the problem, the problem is a phenomenon resulting from student–environment interactions. Traditional approaches to dealing with students who struggle in school have included reducing what is expected of them with curriculum modifications. RTI methods call for a different problem-solving approach in which each student's response to specific teaching procedures is tracked with *data* and reviewed *systematically* to determine whether other instruction is needed. Certainly there are educators already using some, or all, components of the RTI method. However, in order for RTI to be maximally effective for all students, all educators must understand and employ consistent procedures (Brown-Chidsey, Loughlin, & O'Reilly, 2004).

PERSONNEL INVOLVED IN RTI PRACTICES

The universal and general education-based features of RTI mean that all those who work in schools will need to know and use certain RTI elements in their daily activities. The first and most important personnel to implement RTI steps are classroom teachers. For this reason, it is crucial that all of the teachers in every school building have access to training and support for RTI methods. Ideally, such training is provided on a continual basis with ongoing support and consultation. When possible, providing teachers of common grades and subjects the opportunity to learn, discuss, and consult with each other about specific RTI steps is very beneficial. For example, if the first-grade Tier 1 reading curriculum is to be implemented with fidelity and consistency, all of the first-grade teachers need to have the chance to learn about it, practice using it, and communicate with one another about problems and successes they encounter while using it.

Inherent in the RTI model is an expectation that not all students will respond successfully to all Tier 1 instruction. That means Tier 2 interventions need to be available and ready to implement when data reveal that certain students need other interventions. One important question that school-based instructional design teams need to address is "Who will implement Tier 2 instruction?" In an ideal world, general education classroom teachers are the best people to organize, teach, and evaluate Tier 2 instruction. Such procedures could include use of classwide groupings of students for specific instructional activities. Classes might have between 3 and 5 subgroups of students who work together to learn and master specific skills. The teacher would work with each group every day for a brief period of time (no more than 15 minutes) and then move on to the next group. Some teachers have reported that this group-based model will not work because of the highly complex needs of specific students. They worry about whether the other students can manage themselves when the teacher is working with one group at a time. Recognition, anticipation, and planning for the behavior management components of RTI is important. Any RTI implementation plan must include behavior expectations and contingencies for what will happen when students are disruptive.

Due to concerns about classroom behavior management as well as the complex needs of students, some RTI applications have included use of paraprofessionals for Tier 2 instruction. When Tier 2 activities are carried out by paraprofessionals or specialists, the application of RTI methods may not appear to be significantly different from previous student support methods. For example, in schools receiving Title I funds to improve students' reading and math skills, existing paraprofessionals in the form of Title I instructors could implement Tier 2 instruction. If someone other than the classroom teacher implements Tier 2 activities, there must be close and careful communication between these personnel so that all instruction is linked and complementary.

The actual location of Tier 2 instruction is another consideration. The RTI model conceptualizes Tier 2 activities as general education-based instruction. Still, in some schools, the size and arrangement of classroom space makes it all but impossible for small groups to meet in the general classroom. For this reason, it may be best for Tier 2 instruction to occur in a space other than the general classroom. Alternative locations include small special-purpose rooms and offices, anterooms, libraries, and sometimes hallways. Given that the students who receive Tier 2 instruction are among those most at risk in the school, careful consideration of where to hold sessions is needed. Ideal locations are those where students can gather quickly and with minimal transition delay, where necessary materials can be stored and retrieved easily, and where there are minimal distractions and interruptions. In classrooms where setting up a permanent Tier 2 station is possible, this option is recommended so that there is as little interruption in the instructional flow as possible. Having such small-group Tier 2 dedicated space allows the general educator to participate in and/or observe Tier 2 instruction while achieving the goal of truly general classroom multi-tiered intervention.

TRAINING COMPONENTS

In order to increase the likelihood that RTI methods will be successful for students, a planned and sequenced program of teacher training is needed. We recommend that administrative and training personnel develop a specific RTI training plan that includes three main elements: (1) a schedule, (2) teacher learning outcomes, and (3) indicators of teachers' mastery of RTI methods. Each of these will be described in turn. Following these descriptions is a set of overhead slides that trainers can use as part of their training sessions.

Schedule

In order to prepare all teachers for the training and implementation activities, a preset schedule is suggested. The schedule should indicate the location, times, topics, and duration of all planned RTI training sessions. As was noted in Chapter 6, in order to learn anything a certain amount of practice is needed. For this reason multiple training sessions conducted over a period of time are essential. The first session is usually the longest, as it needs to cover a number of conceptual as well as procedural components. For this reason, we suggest that at least one full day be set aside for the initial RTI training session. Subsequent sessions can be about a half-day in length and should cover more detailed aspects of RTI methods. Table 11.1 presents a sample RTI training schedule for the first part of a school year. The training sessions start with everyone participating in a general overview of the RTI plans for the elementary grades. This is important because overall implementation is likely to be more effective if everyone in the school knows what is planned and expected.

After a general session for all staff is completed, more detailed sessions about specific RTI components should be held. For example, if a school will be implementing RTI for math in a given year, then training those staff members who will be responsible for carrying out each stage of the RTI procedures is needed. As shown in Table 11.1, sessions for the classroom teachers to learn how to teach with the new math curriculum are needed. Similarly, the teachers will need to know how and when to conduct the benchmark test-

TABLE 11.1. Sample RTI Training Schedule

Date/time	Location	Topic(s)	People
September 1, 8:30 A.M.–3:30 P.M.	Primary school library	RTI method overview and district implementation plans	All K–5 teachers and staff
September 2, noon–3:00 P.M.	Grade 1 pod	Using the new grade 1 math curriculum: timeframe and expectations	All grade 1 teachers
September 10, noon–3:30 P.M.	Primary school library	Math CBM benchmarking procedures	All K–3 teachers
September 12, 8:30 A.M.–noon	Primary school conference room	Great Leaps for Math training and implementation integrity	All grade 1 Title I math instructors
September 24, noon–3:00 P.M.	Grade-level pods	Understanding CBM math benchmark scores and identifying students needing Tier 2 math instruction	All K–2 teachers and staff in grade-level groups

ing with all students. There should be separate sessions for the curriculum and benchmark training. While these activities are both crucial stages of RTI activities, as teachers are learning to do them, instruction and practice of each part separately is needed. Separate sessions allow for application of the principles of effective instruction that are discussed in Chapter 6. If personnel other than classroom teachers will be implementing specific RTI steps (e.g., Tier 2) then those staff people need training as well. Again, having such training occur in a dedicated manner where the specific skills can be learned, practiced, and reviewed is very important.

Learning Outcomes

Integrated within the training sessions there should be clear and observable learning outcomes. Learning outcomes are the knowledge and skills that the teachers and other staff members will possess as a result of participating in the training sessions. Just as it is important to measure and monitor pupil progress, measuring teachers' RTI skills development is crucial. If teachers and other staff never learn to use the specific instructional and measurement activities included in RTI, it can never truly be implemented. For this reason, each training session should have one or more specific training objectives framed as learning outcomes. Most educators are familiar with the use of such objectives, and they are often included in advertising and evaluation materials for professional development activities. Such outcomes often begin with the phrase "As a result of participating in this workshop, participants will . . ." RTI trainings should be no different, and specific outcomes for every session should be described at the beginning and end of each activity. Examples of RTI learning outcomes are included in Table 11.2. These examples all relate to RTI for math and cover the RTI components needed for successful use of RTI implementation.

TABLE 11.2. Sample RTI Learning Outcomes and Indicators of Mastery

Learning outcome	Indicator of mastery
Knowledge of the core RTI principles and components	Completion of RTI training posttest
Knowledge and skills necessary for using the core (Tier 1) curricula with 100% implementation accuracy (integrity)	Self-report and observer report treatment integrity checklists showing all intervention steps completed accurately
Skills for administration, scoring, and interpretation of benchmarks for basic academic skills	Submission of benchmark scores for all students in a class; creation and implementation of Tier 2 intervention groups
Knowledge and skills necessary for using the Tier 2 instructional materials with 90% or better implementation accuracy (integrity)	Self-report and observer report treatment integrity checklists showing all intervention steps completed accurately
Knowledge and skills necessary for weekly progress monitoring of students receiving Tier 2 instruction	Completion of progress monitoring graphs and review worksheets for all Tier 2 students

Indicators of Mastery

In order to know whether the training participants have achieved the desired outcomes, some form of measurement is needed. This situation is no different from the measurements needed as part of RTI activities with pupils. There are two main ways that teacher and staff mastery of RTI knowledge and skills can be documented: self-report and observation. Ideally, both forms of review will be utilized. If teachers develop the habit of checking their own implementation accuracy as part of the RTI procedures, then completing self-reports of their work will seem natural. Table 11.2 includes mastery indicators matched to the learning outcomes described above. In general, indicators of mastery should be as simple as possible and yet provide lasting evidence that specific procedures and steps were implemented as intended. As was noted in Chapter 7, it is impossible to know the true effectiveness of an intervention if it is implemented incorrectly. For this reason, using intervention integrity checklists and observations is an important part of overall RTI implementation. As noted, if teachers integrate use of such integrity measures into their general RTI practices, the self-reports and observations will not seem intrusive. For this reason, teaching about intervention integrity as part of training is important.

TRAINING SLIDES

The remaining pages of this chapter include reproducible overhead slides that can be used in RTI training sessions. These slides and additional training materials may also be downloaded for PowerPoint presentations from The Guilford Press website at www.guilford.com/rti/.

What Is Response to Intervention?

- Response to Intervention (RTI) is a systematic and data-based method for identifying, defining, and resolving students' academic and/or behavioral difficulties.

Key RTI Features

- Prevention-based model
  —Primary—before any problems exist
  —Secondary—at the first sign of problems
  —Tertiary—to reduce effects of problems
- Includes three elements:
  —Effective instruction
  —Data recording
  —Systematic review of data to inform instruction

RTI Is a *Well-Child* Program for Education

- Health Care
  - —Infant screenings
  - —Annual check-ups
  - —Comparison to developmental standards
  - —Immunizations
  - —Use of research-based standard protocol treatments for common problems
  - —Hypothesis testing as part of evaluation
  - —Referral for specialist care if needed

- Education
  - —Standardized kindergarten screening
  - —Three yearly "check-ups"
  - —Comparison to local and national benchmarks
  - —Use of research-based instruction for general education instruction
  - —Hypothesis testing as part of curriculum and assessment practices
  - —Referral to special education only if progress in other instruction is not made

RTI Stages

- Usually conceptualized as a multi-tier (stage) model in which students get more individualized assistance on the basis of whether they respond to certain instruction.
- Three-tier model is most common.
- Outcome indicators are essential to determine whether the students have responded to the instruction.

Three-Tier RTI Model

- Tier 1
  —Scientifically based general education instruction with regular progress monitoring
- Tier 2
  —Intensive small-group scientifically based instruction with regular progress monitoring
- Tier 3
  —Comprehensive evaluation for special education services using a problem-solving model

Three Tiers of Instruction

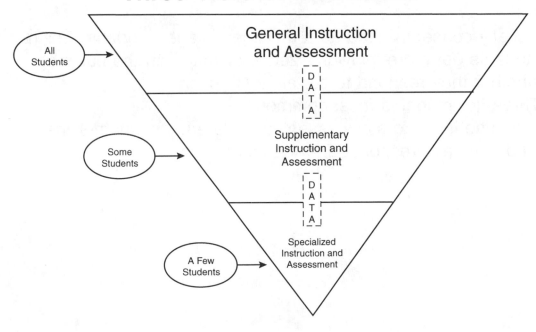

RTI Research

- Majority of data are related to reading.
- Data indicate that using RTI procedures optimizes outcomes for all students.
- Studies show that not all students will be successful from RTI alone; those students who still struggle need to receive special education services.
- Learning disabilities do exist and will not be eradicated with RTI policies.

RTI and Education Policies

- RTI procedures are specifically mentioned in both NCLB and IDEIA 2004.
- IDEIA 2004 requires that students receive scientifically based instruction before special education referrals can be made.
- RTI data can be used as part of the evaluation procedures for determining the presence of a specific learning disability.

Research on RTI and Special Education Services

- RTI has been shown to reduce the number of students identified as LD (Marston, Muyskens, Lau, & Canter, 2003).
- RTI also has been linked with a drop in the overall number of special education placements (O'Connor, 2003).
- RTI led to a significant reduction in primary grades special education referrals and placement when used specifically for early intervention (K–3) programming (Tilly, 2003).
- RTI does not eliminate or discount the presence of LD, but is one important step in the process toward diagnosis and treatment (Speece, Case, & Molloy, 2003).

Why Use Response to Intervention?

- There is clear evidence that RTI methods have helped promote better reading intervention practices.
- RTI appears to help build a bridge between general and special education by offering decision-making tools and opportunities for communication about, and ownership of, children's learning experiences.
- RTI procedures offer "well-child" prevention-focused methods for education.
- RTI policies are linked with a reduction in the number of students receiving special education.

RTI Components: Tier 1

Tier 1 RTI Activities:
   —Whole-class reading instruction using research-based curriculum.
   —Oral reading fluency benchmarks to monitor student progress three times per year.
   —Identification of the lowest 20%.
   —Comparison with teacher judgment.

- Next step: Tier 2

RTI Components: Tier 2

- Tier 2 activities:
   —Daily small-group instruction in addition to whole-class instruction (added reading instruction).
   —Direct and systematic instruction in the core reading skills that students need.
   —Monitor student progress using DIBELS and/or CBM.
   —Those students still not meeting benchmark goals at preset time points are referred for special education evaluation.

- Next Step: Tier 3

RTI Components: Tier 3

- Tier 3 activities:
  —Review of Tier 2 data.
  —Comprehensive evaluation to identify why student has not responded to intervention.
  —Consideration of special education eligibility.
  —Development of IEP or other intervention.
  —Ongoing progress monitoring.

RTI in 10 Easy Steps

- There are 10 basic steps to designing and implementing RTI procedures in a school.
- Each step is essential and will affect the overall quality of the process and data collected.
- The steps need to be implemented in order.
- See page 64 and Form 7.1.

RTI Step 1

- Implement scientifically based general education instructional methods.
- Scientifically based instruction includes those methods shown to result in better outcomes for students in multiple research studies.
- Review of evidence to support specific curricula needs to be conducted before selecting instructional materials and methods.
- Evaluation of the integrity (accuracy) of Tier 1 interventions needs to be conducted regularly.
- See pages 64–67, Forms 7.2 and 7.3, and Figures 7.1 and 7.2.

RTI Step 2

- Collect benchmarks of all students' performance three times during the school year:
  —Fall (September 15–October 15)
  —Winter (January 1–31)
  —Spring (May 1–31)
- See pages 67–73, Forms 7.4 and 7.5, and Figures 7.3 and 7.4.

RTI Step 3

- Identify which students scored below the benchmark target(s).
- Those students below the target are at risk for significant school difficulties.
- Compare the at-risk student list with teacher judgment and other indicators of students' progress.
- See pages 73–75, Form 7.6, and Figure 7.5.

RTI Step 4

- Provide daily scientifically based small-group instruction to students with scores below benchmark target(s) for at least 3 weeks.
- Just like general interventions, the specialized ones need to be scientifically based and supported with evidence.
- See pages 75–81, Form 7.7, and Figure 7.6.

RTI Step 5

- Monitor student progress toward the benchmark(s), using daily assessments and data graphing for 3 school weeks.
- Frequent assessment of student progress has been shown to be important for effective instructional decision making.
- Students need to see the data too.
- See pages 81–83, Form 7.8, and Figure 7.7.

RTI Step 6

- Review, revise, and/or discontinue small-group instruction based on student performance and progress toward the benchmark at the end of 3 weeks.
- Interventions should not last forever and need to be reviewed frequently.
- The data tell the story.
- See page 84, Form 7.10, and Figures 7.8 and 7.10.

RTI Step 7

- For students not yet showing evidence of meeting the benchmark(s) by the end of the first 3 weeks, increase the intensity, duration, and/or frequency of instruction and continue to monitor progress for up to another 3 weeks.
- Every effort to help the student find success is needed.
- See pages 84–85, Form 7.9, and Figure 7.9.

RTI Step 8

- Review, revise, and/or discontinue small-group instruction, based on student performance and attainment of benchmark at the end of the second 3 weeks.
- It's important to keep records of progress reviews.
- See page 85 and Figures 7.9 and 7.10.

RTI Step 9

- For students not yet showing evidence of meeting the benchmark(s) by the end of the school year, initiate a comprehensive evaluation to determine whether the student has a disability and is eligible for special education services.
- Intervention continues during evaluation.
- See page 85, Form 7.11, and Figure 7.11.

RTI Step 10

- IEP team determines whether student has a disability and meets the criteria for special education services; if the student is eligible for special education, an IEP is developed and becomes the student's new instructional program.
- For students found not eligible other solutions must be tried.
- See pages 85–87.

Summary

- RTI appears to offer a robust and technically sound set of methods that enhance student achievement while reducing special education placements.
- RTI appears to be a viable way to improve access to effective instruction for all students.
- RTI is not a replacement for all other assessment procedures but a set of procedures that make educational planning easier.

12

Frequently Asked Questions
. . . and Our Best Responses

Some Conclusions about RTI

This chapter includes a number of frequently asked questions about RTI, followed by our answers to these questions. Where applicable, we refer readers to the page numbers were more elaborate answers to the question may be found.

1. *What is response to intervention?* *Response to intervention* (RTI) is a systematic and data-based method for identifying, defining, and resolving students' academic and/or behavioral difficulties (see pp. 3–4 in Chapter 1). We have defined RTI as a general set of procedures that can be applied to the specific needs of students in schools. While this book focuses on how RTI procedures can be used in relation to academic skill development, RTI methods are applicable to the assessment of students with problem behavior as well.

2. *What does the recent reauthorization of IDEIA say about RTI?* The 2004 version of the Individuals with Disabilities Education Improvment Act (IDEIA) specifically includes RTI methods. As described in more detail on pages 23–24 of Chapter 3, IDEIA 2004 calls for the verification that a student has received scientifically based instruction in reading and/or math before being identified as a student with a specific learning disability. Additionally, RTI procedures are included in IDEIA 2004 as an allowable component of the assessment methods used to determine whether a student has a specific learning disability.

3. *We've been using a discrepancy model for identifying students with learning disabilities for years. What's the problem with continuing to use this model?* A number of limitations to the widely used IQ–achievement discrepancy formula for identifying learning disabilities have been documented. Chapter 3 of this volume describes these limitations (pp. 21–22). A brief summary of the research is that IQ–achievement discrepancy formulas are very inaccurate. Given that the goal of special education is to provide chil-

dren with disabilities a free, appropriate education in the least restrictive environment, continuing to use a discrepancy formula known to be inaccurate in determining which students have a learning disability does not fulfill the mission of special education. Some research has shown that use of discrepancy formulas has led to *more restrictive* educational placements for students. Continuing to use a discrepancy formula when more accurate and less restrictive methods are available is not justified.

4. *How does RTI compare with curriculum-based measurement procedures?* RTI involves using a wide array of assessment and instructional methods. In contrast, curriculum-based measurement (CBM) is one specific type of assessment that can be used for evaluation of students' academic skills. CBM procedures can be used as part of RTI, but they are not one and the same. CBM and RTI do share a common link with a problem-solving model of assessment, in which students' school difficulties are understood as being manifestations of person–environment interactions. RTI for academic skills may include use of CBM, but will also include many more steps and procedures as well. RTI for problem behaviors would not involve use of CBM, but might include use of Functional Behavioral Assessment (FBA) procedures.

5. *Does this mean no more IQ testing?* Maybe. But probably not. Although the limitations of IQ scores have been described by many authors over time (Brown-Chidsey, 2005a; Gould, 1981/1996), they are not likely to disappear immediately. As noted above, there are significant problems with IQ–achievement score discrepancies, but this is different from problems with IQ scores themselves. Research has shown that IQ scores do provide a general indicator of cognitive ability after about the age of 10 and over the lifespan. At this time, an IQ score is still required for diagnosis of mental retardation; thus, IQ tests will continue to be used for the foreseeable future for certain assessments. Additionally, certain components of IQ tests may be useful for detailed testing of specific cognitive abilities (Flanagan & Harrison, 2005).

6. *How time consuming is this method?* When compared with the 10 or more hours often estimated to go into each individualized evaluation conducted for special education eligibility, RTI procedures are really not time-consuming at all. While the research steps necessary to review potential Tier 1 and 2 interventions may take several hours, the benchmark testing is very brief, taking about 10 minutes per student at the longest. If CBM is used as the benchmark data collection tool, the only measures requiring individualized testing are DIBELS and oral reading fluency. In the areas of math, spelling, and writing, the assessment items can be administered to entire classes at a time. Similarly, CBM progress-monitoring procedures are very fast, involving weekly testing of 2 minutes or less per student.

Importantly, several studies (Fuchs, Mick, Morgan, & Young, 2003; O'Connor, 2003; Tilly, 2003) have shown that RTI methods reduce the overall number of comprehensive evaluations needed, so there is a replacement of personnel time rather than an increase in staffing. Specific data on how many hours expended on specific RTI procedures need to be collected so that comparisons and cost effectiveness can be calculated. There are provisions in IDEIA 2004 for use of a certain amount of special education funds for joint general–special education services and instruction. Specifically, schools districts can spend up to 15% of their special education (IDEIA) money on activities that include general education students. Ideal uses for the 15% allocation include materials, training, and support for Tier 2 interventions. Tier 1 activities are clearly general education programs; however, Tier 2 is designed to provide prevention-focused programs for students who are at risk for school difficulties. If most of the students who receive Tier 2 supports never need special education, then both the 15% money as well as cost savings from reductions in the number of students with disabilities can be used to fund and strengthen Tier 2 programs and consultation activities by school psychology personnel that support such interventions. Since school psychologists are among the best-trained people for designing, monitoring, and supervising RTI activities, a long-term need for all current, as well as additional, school psychology practitioners is expected.

7. *Is RTI useful with general education students or just students with learning disabilities?* RTI procedures help *all students*. RTI is a general education methodology designed to enhance educational outcomes for all students. Students with learning disabilities are frequently mentioned in RTI research, because they make up the largest subgroup of students with disabilities. Nonetheless, RTI methods have been shown to help a wide range of students, regardless of disability.

8. *Does RTI result in an increase in identification of LD students?* No. Data collected so far have shown that RTI procedures are associated with a decrease in the number of students identified as learning disabled. Analysis of these data suggest that such reductions are the result of providing students preventive services so that the actual incidence of LD is reduced. This phenomenon is similar to prevention efforts in healthcare wherein healthy lifestyle factors such as good nutrition and exercise can reduce the actual incidence of such conditions as obesity, diabetes, and hypertension. Some students will still manifest learning disabilities, but the overall numbers are expected to decrease if specific instructional methods are applied at critical early grade levels.

9. *Will this model result in the reduction of school psychology positions?* Not necessarily. Although data pertaining to personnel and staffing for RTI have yet to be reported, evidence from districts where it has been implemented already has not shown any decrease in school psychology positions. Indeed, in certain localities, the number of school psychologists has actually increased when RTI methods have been put into place. Such new jobs become possible when RTI procedures result in fewer special education placements and money can be reallocated from evaluation to prevention and consultation services. These additional school psychology staff members can then help maintain the benefits obtained through RTI methods.

10. *What resources are available to support those of us who need additional training in the use of RTI methods?* In addition to this book, a number of RTI training resources exist. Professional associations such as the Council for Exceptional Children, National Association of School Psychologists, National Education Association, and others have materials about RTI methods. State and regional associations also offer workshops and training each year; as RTI is implemented, it is expected that such workshops will include RTI training opportunities. The U.S. Department of Education has set up a website specifically for information about evidence-based education practices. Known as the What Works Clearinghouse (www.whatworks.ed.gov), this resource provides a continuously updated source for information on scientifically based instructional practices.

Similarly, the Institute for the Development of Educational Achievement at the University of Oregon (idea.uoregon.edu) offers research summaries and technical assistance focusing on education attainment for all students.

11. *What is the role of general education teachers in using RTI?* General educators are the "first-line" personnel in RTI. They welcome, work with, and know the challenges facing students from the moment they come to school. For this reason, RTI is first—and foremost—a general education initiative. That means that general education teachers have a critical role in making RTI work. Indeed, more general educators will be involved in RTI than all the specialists combined. For this reason, it is essential that training, materials, and support for general education teachers be integrated into all RTI planning from the very beginning. Chapter 11 provides RTI training materials that can be used to prepare all teachers, specialists, and others to implement RTI procedures.

12. *If IDEIA 2004 does not require use of RTI, why should I use it?* First, it's the right thing to do. A plethora of evidence has documented how past and current special education programs are not meeting students needs. RTI has been shown to provide an effective mechanism by which students can receive the instruction they need. The old adage "If it's not broke, don't fix it" does not apply here. There is clear evidence that both general and special education programs in many parts of the United States are broken and need to be fixed. RTI offers a way to repair and improve instruction for all students. Just because IDEIA 2004 recommends but does not (yet) require RTI does not excuse professionals who know of its benefits from applying the three tiers to improve educational outcomes for students.

BENEFITS OF RTI

This book has provided a detailed description of the research, model, and steps relating to response-to-intervention methods. Although RTI is still an emerging methodology, we believe that it offers great promise for increasing the likelihood that *all* students will be successful in school.

PRINCIPLES, SKILLS, AND PRACTICES

RTI is composed of principles, skills, and practices. Alone, each of these components is a modestly useful pedagogical tool. For example, the RTI principle of data-driven systematic instruction can be useful to teachers outside of RTI activities in that it provides a way to organize and structure classroom activities. Similarly, the skills necessary to implement RTI such as benchmark collection and data interpretation can help teachers review their own past or current assessment and instruction practices. Likewise, applying RTI methods such as creating Tier 2 groups may be helpful for certain students. It is the combination of all three components that makes RTI truly useful. As noted at the beginning of this volume, RTI borrows from a number of scientifically based educational practices that have long been shown to be effective. By combining these techniques, RTI offers a comprehensive, prevention-oriented approach to maximizing learning for all students.

RTI APPLICATIONS

There are two major subdivisions into which RTI can be organized. First and foremost it is a general education initiative designed to promote the most effective instruction for all students. Second, RTI provides a set of procedures that can be used in conjunction with other evaluation tools to identify whether a student has a specific learning disability.

General Education

When used as part of general education, RTI has several distinct advantages. First, RTI facilitates greater communication and consistency across those who teach the same grade or subject. While teachers may share ideas and plans with one another on a collegial basis, there is not a strong history of systematic discussion of progress for all students in the same grade. Second, RTI procedures place emphasis on a belief that all students can learn. By providing all students with high-quality systematic instruction and monitoring their progress, the RTI methodology assumes that most students will be successful. Importantly, even those students who need the extra instruction provided in Tier 2 lessons are included in general education. The goal and expectation is that all students can learn if given the right instruction. A small number of students will not respond to Tier 2 instruction, and comprehensive evaluation of their needs may result in special education services. Still, the mantra covering all aspects of RTI is that students who are not successful at a given tier are those students for whom the right (i.e., effective) intervention has not *yet* been found.

Special Education

RTI also has a role in special education. Specifically, it is mentioned in IDEIA 2004 as one of several assessment tools that can be combined to determine whether a student has a learning disability. The nature of the RTI wording in IDEIA documents a strong message that the least restrictive environment (LRE) is an important aspect of educational planning for all students. A similar emphasis is found in the No Child Left Behind Act. Both IDEIA (2004) and NCLB include language requiring that schools do everything in their power to provide all students with high-quality scientifically based effective instruction. Legislative mandates requiring certain procedures are not the same thing as the actual application of the procedures. Only time will tell how well the goals stated in IDEIA and NCLB are met. Still, the policy emphasis is clear: as a society we must do *everything* we can to educate *all* students in certain basic skills. Less explicit in the laws and regulations is the rationale for this universal policy. Unstated is the critical importance of basic skills in reading, writing, and mathematics for basic economic sufficiency.

Certainly some critics might argue about the merit of this emphasis; however, the emerging economic trends in most world regions support attainment of basic educational skills by all students, or at least as many as possible.

FUTURE DIRECTIONS

Every scientific endeavor requires ongoing research. Even among the most validated and documented practices, scientists continue to refine and verify prior findings. When a body of knowledge is no longer studied, it is no longer scientific. The same is true for educational sciences. More study of all aspects of RTI is needed. A variety of research strands need to be explored. However, the three main questions about RTI of greatest urgency are:

1. What are the long-term student outcomes when RTI methods are used?
2. Are there differences in outcomes when RTI methods are used with students from diverse linguistic, racial, religious, cultural, disability and regional groups?
3. What are the organizational and systems variables needed to promote and sustain effective RTI practices?

RTI researchers are urged to address these questions as part of their scientific endeavors. Other questions will emerge as a result of ongoing RTI practices and research. Only through systematic and long-term investigation will the ultimate relative value and importance of RTI be realized. While such work is ongoing, all educators are encouraged to learn, use, and evaluate those RTI practices specific to their area(s), using the obtained student data to promote academic success for all students.

References

Ackerman, R. D. (1987). Regular education initiative [Letter to the Editor]. *Journal of Learning Disabilities, 20*, 514–515.

American Academy of Child and Adolescent Psychiatry. (1993, October 20). Policy statement on facilitated communication. Retrieved from www.aacap.org/publications/policy

American Academy of Pediatrics, Committee on Children with Disabilities. (1998). Auditory Integration Training and Facilitated Communication for Autism. *Pediatrics, 102*, 431–433.

American Association on Mental Retardation. (2005). Behavioral supports [position statement]. Retrieved from www.aamr.org/Policies/pos_beh_sppts.shtml

American Psychological Association. (1994). Resolution facilitated communication. Retrieved from www.apa.org/about/division/cpmscientific.html#6

American Speech–Language–Hearing Association. (1994). Technical report of the subcommittee on facilitated communication of the ad hoc committee on auditory integration training and facilitated communication. Retrieved from www.asha.org/NR/rdonlyres/08EAEF85-0EEC-49DF-A4FA-B8F295D6B6DD/0/19454_1.pdf

Association for Behavior Analysis. (1995). *Position statement on students' right to effective education.* Retrieved from www.abainternational.org/sub/membersvcs/journals-pubs/pssree/index.asp

August, D., & Hakuta, K. (Eds.). (1997). *Improving schooling for language minority children: A research agenda.* Washington, DC: National Academy Press.

Bagnato, S. J., & Neisworth, J. T. (1991). *Assessment for early intervention: Best practices for professionals.* New York: Guilford Press.

Baker, S., Plasencia-Peinado, J., & Lezcano-Lytle, V. (1998). The use of curriculum-based measurement with language minority students. In M. R. Shinn (Ed.), *Advanced applications of curriculum-based measurement* (pp. 175–213). New York: Guilford Press.

Berg, W., Wacker, D., & Steege, M. (1995). Best practices in the assessment with persons who have severe or profound handicaps. In A. Thomas & J. Grimes (Eds.), *Best practices in school psychology* (pp. 805–816). Washington, DC: National Association of School Psychologists.

Blachman, B. A., Fletcher, J. M., Schatschneider, C., Francis, D. J., Clonan, S. M., Shaywitz, B. A., & Shaywitz, S. E. (2004). Effects of intensive reading remediation for second and third graders and a 1-year follow-up. *Journal of Educational Psychology, 96*, 444–462.

Biglan, A., Mrazek, P. J., Carnine, D., & Flay, B. R. (2003). The integration of research and practice in the prevention of youth problem behaviors. *American Psychologist, 58,* 433–441.

Boscardin, M. L., Brown-Chidsey, R. , & Gonzalez-Martinez, J. (2002a). Assessment of children from diverse backgrounds. In J. Carey & P. Pedersen (Eds.), *Multicultural counseling in the schools* (2nd ed., pp. 257–279). Boston: Allyn & Bacon.

Boscardin, M. L., Brown-Chidsey, R. & Gonzalez-Martinez, J. (2002b). The essential link for students with disabilities from diverse backgrounds: Forging partnerships with families. *Journal of Special Education Leadership, 14,* 89–95.

Bransford, J. D. (1979). *Human cognition: Learning, understanding, and remembering.* Belmont, CA: Wadsworth.

Bransford, J. D., Brown, A. L., & Cocking, R. R. (Eds.). (2000). *How people learn: Brain, mind experience, and school* (expanded ed.). Washington, DC: National Academy Press.

Brown, G. W., & Brown, C. V. (2005). Physiological factors in students' school success. In R. Brown-Chidsey (Ed.), *Assessment for intervention: A problem-solving approach* (pp. 103–128). New York: Guilford Press.

Brown-Chidsey, R. (2005a). Intelligence tests in an era of standards-based educational reform. In D. P. Flanagan & P. L. Harrison (Eds.), *Contemporary intellectual assessment: Theories, tests, and issues* (2nd ed., pp. 631–641). New York: Guilford Press.

Brown-Chidsey, R. (2005b). Introduction to problem-solving assessment. In R. Brown-Chidsey (Ed.), *Assessment for intervention: A problem-solving approach* (pp. 3–9). New York: Guilford Press.

Brown-Chidsey, R. (2005c). Scaling educational assessments to inform instruction for all students: Response to intervention as essential educational science. *Trainer's Forum, 24,* 1–4, 6–8.

Brown-Chidsey, R., Davis, L., & Maya, C. (2003). Sources of variance in curriculum-based measures of silent reading. *Psychology in the Schools, 40,* 363–377.

Brown-Chidsey, R., Loughlin, J. E., & O'Reilly, M. J. (2004, April). *Using response to intervention methods with struggling learners.* Mini-Skills Presentation at the annual meeting of the National Association of School Psychologists, Dallas, TX.

Brown-Chidsey, R., Seppala, M., & Segura, M. L. (2000). Chapter 766: Massachusetts special education law. *American Education Annual.* New York: Gale.

Brown-Chidsey, R., & Steege, M. W. (2005). Solution-focused psychoeducational reports. In R. Brown-Chidsey (Ed.), *Assessment for intervention: A problem-solving approach* (pp. 267–290). New York: Guilford Press.

Bryan, T., Bay, M., & Donahue, M. (1988). Implications of the learning disabilities definition for the regular education initiative. *Journal of Learning Disabilities, 21,* 23–28.

Burns, M. K. (2002). Comprehensive system of assessment to intervention using curriculum-based assessments. *Intervention in School and Clinic, 38,* 8–13.

Caplan, G. (1964). *Principles of Preventive Psychiatry.* New York: Basic Books.

Carnine, D. (1981). Reducing training problems associated with visually and auditorily similar correspondences. *Journal of Learning Disabilities, 14,* 276–279.

Carnine, D. (1989). Designing practice activities. *Journal of Learning Disabilities, 22,* 603–607.

Carnine, D. (1997a). Bridging the research-to-practice gap. *Exceptional Children, 63,* 513–524.

Carnine, D. (1997b). Instructional design for students with learning disabilities. *Journal of Learning Disabilities, 30,* 130–142.

Carnine, D., & Carnine, L. (2004). The interaction of reading skills and science content knowledge when teaching struggling secondary students. *Reading and Writing Quarterly, 20,* 203–219.

Carnine, D., & Gersten, R. (2000). The nature and roles of research in improving achievement in mathematics. *Journal for Research in Mathematics Education, 31,* 138–142.

Carnine, D., & Granzin, A. (2001). Setting learning expectations for students with disabilities. *School Psychology Review, 30,* 466–472.

Carnine, D., & Jitendra, A. K. (1997). A descriptive analysis of mathematics curricular materials from a pedagogical perspective. *Remedial & Special Education, 18,* 66–82.

Carnine, D., Kame'enui, E., & Maggs, A. (1982). Components of analytic assistance: Statement saying, concept training, and strategy training. *Journal of Educational Research, 75,* 375–377.

Carter, R. T., Helms, J. E., & Juby, H. L. (2004). The relationship between racism and racial identity for white Americans: A profile analysis. *Journal of Multicultural Counseling and Development, 32,* 2–18.

Cartledge, G. (1996). *Cultural diversity and social skills instruction: Understanding ethnic and gender differences.* Champaign, IL: Research Press.

Case, L. P., Speece, D. L., & Molloy, D. E. (2003). The validity of a response-to-instruction paradigm to identify reading disabilities: A longitudinal analysis of individual differences and contextual factors. *School Psychology Review, 32,* 557–582.

Center for Academic and Reading Skills, University of Texas–Houston Health Science Center, Texas Institute for Measurement, Evaluation, and Statistics, University of Houston. (1999). *Technical report: Texas primary reading inventory.* Retrieved October 12, 2004, from www.tpri.org.

Chall, J. S. (2000). *The academic achievement challenge: What really works in the classroom?* New York: Guilford Press.

Chisholm, D. P. (1988). Concerns respecting the regular education initiative. *Journal of Learning Disabilities, 21,* 487–501.

Coates, R. D. (1989). The regular education initiative and opinions of regular classroom teachers. *Journal of Learning Disabilities, 22,* 532–536.

Cognition and Technology Group at Vanderbilt. (1997). *The Jasper Project: Lessons in curriculum, instruction, assessment, and professional development.* Mahwah, NJ: Erlbaum.

Compton, D. L. (2003, December). *RTI: It's all about the nudge.* Paper presented at the Response-to-Intervention Symposium, Kansas City, MO. Retrieved March 9, 2004, from www.nrcld.org/html/symposium2003

Coyne, M. D., Kame'enui, E. J., & Simmons, D. C. (2004). Improving beginning reading instruction and intervention for students with LD: Reconciling "all" with "each." *Journal of Learning Disabilities, 37,* 231–240.

Coyne, M. D., Kame'enui, E. J., & Simmons, D. C. (2001). Prevention and intervention in beginning reading: Two complex systems. *Learning Disabilities Research and Practice, 16,* 62–74.

Coyne, M. D., Kame'enui, E. J., Simmons, D. C. , & Harn, B. A. (2004). Beginning reading intervention as inoculation or insulin: First-grade reading performance of strong responders to kindergarten intervention. *Journal of Learning Disabilities, 37,* 90–105.

Cummins, J. (1979). Cognitive/academic language proficiency, linguistic interdependence, the optimum age ques\tion and some other matters. *Working Papers on Bilingualism,* No. 19, 121–129.

Cummins, J. (1986) Empowering minority students: A framework for intervention. *Harvard Educational Review, 56,* 18–36.

Cummins, J. (1996) *Negotiating identities: Education for empowerment in a diverse society.* Los Angeles: California Association for Bilingual Education.

D'Alonzo, B. J., & Boggs, E. T. (1990). A review of the regular education initiative. *Preventing School Failure, 35,* 18–24.

Deno, E. (1970). Special education as developmental capital. *Exceptional Children*, 37, 229–237.

Deno, S. L. (2002). Problem solving as "best practice." In A. Thomas & J. Grimes (Eds.), *Best practices in school psychology IV* (pp. 37–56). Bethesda, MD: National Association of School Psychologists.

Deno, S. L. (2005). Problem-solving assessment. In R. Brown-Chidsey (Ed.), *Assessment for intervention: A problem-solving approach* (pp. 10–40). New York: Guilford Press.

Doll, B., & Haack, K. M. (2005). Population-based strategies for identifying schoolwide problems. In R. Brown-Chidsey (Ed.), *Assessment for intervention: A problem-solving approach* (pp. 82–102). New York: Guilford Press.

Drame, E. R. (2002). Sociocultural context effects of teachers' readiness to refer for learning disabilities. *Exceptional Children*, 69, 41–53.

Edformation. (2004). AIMSweb. Retrieved November 8, 2004, from www.edformation.com/.

Elliott, S. N., & Fuchs, L. S. (1997). The utility of curriculum-based measurement and performance assessment as alternatives to traditional intelligence and achievement tests. *School Psychology Review*, 26, 224–233.

Engelmann, S. (1999). The benefits of direct instruction: Affirmative action for at-risk students. *Educational Leadership*, 57, 77–79.

Evans, R. (1990). Making mainstreaming work through prereferral consultation. *Educational Leadership*, 48, 73–78.

Flanagan, D. P., & Harrison, P. L. (Eds.). (2005). *Contemporary intellectual assessment: Theories, tests, and issues* (2nd ed.). New York: Guilford Press.

Flanagan, D. P., & Ortiz, S. (2001). *Essentials of cross-battery assessment*. New York: Wiley.

Fletcher, J. M. (2003, December). *Validity of alternative approaches to the identification of LD: Operationalizing unexpected underachievement*. Paper presented at the Response-to-Intervention Symposium, Kansas City, MO. Retrieved March 9, 2004, from www.nrcld.org/html/symposium2003

Fletcher, J. M., Coulter, W. A., Reschly, D. J., & Vaughn, S. (2004). Alternative approached to the definition and identification of learning disabilities: Some questions and answers. *Annals of Dyslexia*, 54, 304–331.

Fletcher, J. M., Foorman, B. R., Boudousquie, A., Barnes, M. A., Schatschneider, C., & Francis, D. J. (2002). Assessment of reading and learning disabilities: A research-based intervention oriented approach. *Journal of School Psychology*, 40, 27–63.

Fletcher, J. M., Morris, R. D., & Lyon, G. R. (2003). Classification and definition of learning disabilities: An integrative perspective. In H. L. Swanson, K. R. Harris, & S. Graham (Eds.), *Handbook of learning disabilities* (pp. 30–56). New York: Guilford Press.

Foorman, B. R. (2003). *Preventing and remediating reading difficulties: Bringing science to scale*. Baltimore: York Press.

Foorman, B. R., Breier, J. I., & Fletcher, J. M. (2003). Interventions aimed at improving reading success: An evidence-based approach. *Developmental Neuropsychology*, 24, 613–640.

Foxx, R. M. (1999). Long term maintenance of language and social skills. *Behavioral Interventions*, 14, 135–147.

Francis, D. J. (2003, December). *Response to intervention (RTI): A conceptually and statistically superior alternative to discrepancy*. Paper presented at the Response-to-Intervention Symposium,Kansas City, MO. Retrieved March 9, 2004, from www.nrcld.org/html/symposium2003

Freeman P. J. (1994). National health care reform minus public health: A formula for failure. *Public Health Policy*, 15, 261–282.

Fuchs, D. (2003, December). *Responding to nonresponders: An experimental field trial of iden-*

tification and intervention methods. Paper presented at the Response-to-Intervention Symposium, Kansas City, MO. Retrieved March 9, 2004, from www.nrcld.org/html/symposium2003

Fuchs, D., & Fuchs, L. S. (1994). Inclusive schools movement and the radicalization of special education reform. *Exceptional Children, 60,* 294–300.

Fuchs, D., Fuchs, L. S., Mathes, P. G., Lipsey, M. E., & Eaton, S. (2000). A meta-analysis of reading differences between underachievers with and without the disability label: A brief report. *Learning Disabilities, 10,* 1–4.

Fuchs, D., Mick, D., Morgan, P. L., & Young, C. L. (2003). Responsiveness to intervention: Definitions, evidence, and implications for the learning disabilities construct. *Learning Disabilities: Research and Practice, 18,* 157–171.

Fuchs, L. (2003). Assessing intervention responsiveness: Conceptual and technical issues. *Learning Disabilities: Research and Practice, 18,* 172–186.

Fuchs, L. S., & Deno, S. L. (1994). Must instructionally useful assessment be based in the curriculum? *Exceptional Children, 61,* 15–24.

Gersten, R., & Carnine, D. (1986). Direct instruction in reading comprehension. *Educational Leadership, 43,* 70–79.

Gibb, G. S., & Wilder, L. K. (2002). Using functional analysis to improve reading instruction for reading instruction for students with learning disabilities and emotional/behavioral disorders. *Preventing School Failure, 46,* 152–157.

Glutting, J. J., McDermott, P. A., Watkins, M. M., Kush, J. C., & Konold, T. R. (1997). The base rate problem and its consequences for interpreting children's ability profiles. *School Psychology Review, 26,* 176–188.

Good, R. H., & Kaminski, R. A. (Eds.). (2002). *Dynamic Indicators of Basic Early Literacy Skills* (6th ed.). Eugene, OR: Institute for the Development of Educational Achievement. Retrieved November 8, 2004, from dibels.uoregon.edu/

Good, III, R. H., Simmons, D. C., & Kame'enui, E. J. (2001). The importance and decision-making utility of a continuum of fluency-based indicators of foundational reading skills for third-grade high-stakes outcomes. *Scientific Studies of Reading, 5,* 257–289.

Gould, S. J. (1996). *The mismeasure of man.* New York: Norton. (Originally published in 1981)

Graham, S., & Harris, K. R. (1997). It can be taught, but it does not develop naturally: Myths and realities in writing instruction. *School Psychology Review, 26,* 414–425.

Great Leaps Math. (2004). Retrieved November 8, 2004, from www.greatleaps.com

Green, G. (1996). Evaluating claims about treatments for autism. In C. Maurice, G. Green, & S. Luce (Eds.), *Behavioral Intervention For Young Children With Autism: A Manual for Parents and Professionals* (pp. 15–27). Austin, TX: Pro-Ed.

Gutkin, T. B. (2002). Evidence-based interventions in school psychology: State of the art and directions for the future. *School Psychology Quarterly, 17,* 339–340.

Hallahan, D. P., Keller, C. E., McKinney, J. D., Lloyd, J. W., & Bryan, T. (1988). Examining the research base of the regular education initiative: Efficacy studies and the adaptive learning environments model. *Journal of Learning Disabilities, 21,* 29–35, 55.

Halperin, S. (1979). ESEA comes of age: Some historical reflections. *Educational Leadership, 36,* 349–353.

Hart, B., & Risley, T. R. (1995). *Meaningful differences in the everyday experience of young American children.* Baltimore: Brookes.

Hayes, S. C., Barlow, D. H., & Nelson-Grey, R. O. (1999). *The scientist-practitioner: Research and accountability in the age of managed care.* Boston: Allyn & Bacon.

Helms, J. E. (1992). Why is there no study of cultural equivalence in standardized cognitive ability testing? *American Psychologist, 47,* 1083–1102.

Individuals with Disabilities Education Act. (1997). Public Law 105-17.

Individuals with Disabilities Education Improvement Act. (2004). Public Law 108-446 (20 U.S.C. 1400 *et seq.*).

Institute of Medicine (U.S.), Committee on the Evaluation of Vaccine Purchase Financing in the United States. (2004). *Financing vaccines in the 21st century: Assuring access and availability.* Washington, DC: National Academies Press.

Jenkins, J. R., Pious, C. G., & Jewell, M. (1990). Special education and the regular education initiative: Basic assumptions. *Exceptional Children, 56*(6), 479–491.

Kame'enui, E. J., & Carnine, D. W. (1998). *Effective teaching strategies that accommodate diverse learners.* Upper Saddle River, NJ: Merrill.

Kame'enui, E. J., & Simmons, D. (2002). *Early reading intervention.* Upper Saddle River, NJ: Pearson/Scott Foresman.

Kaminski, R. A., & Good, R. H., III. (1998). Assessing early literacy skills in a problem-solving model: Dynamic Indicators of Basic Early Literacy Skills. In M. R. Shinn (Ed.), *Advanced applications of curriculum-based measurement* (pp. 113–142). New York: Guilford Press.

Kavale, K. A. (2001). Decision making in special education: The function of meta-analysis. *Exceptionality, 9,* 245–269.

Kavale, K. A. (2002). Mainstreaming to full inclusion: From orthogenesis to pathogenesis of an idea. *International Journal of Disability, Development and Education, 49,* 201–215.

Kavale, K. A. (2003, December). The feasibility of a responsiveness to intervention approach for the identification of specific learning disability: A psychometric alternative. Paper presented at the Response-to-Intervention Symposium, Kansas City, MO. Retrieved March 9, 2004, from www.nrcld.org/html/symposium2003

Kavale, K. A., & Forness, S. R. (2000). History, rhetoric, and reality. *Remedial and Special Education, 21,* 279–297.

Klein, W. (2004). *Toward humanity and justice: The writings of Kenneth B. Clark, scholar of the 1954 Brown v. Board of Education decision.* New York: Praeger.

Kovaleski, J. F. (2003, December). The three-tier model for identifying learning disabilities: Critical program features and system issues. Paper presented at the Response-to-Intervention Symposium, Kansas City, MO. Retrieved March 9, 2004, from www.nrcld.org/html/symposium2003

Kranzler, J. H. (1997). Educational and policy issues related to the use and interpretation of intelligence tests in the schools. *School Psychology Review, 26,* 150–163.

Kratochwill, T. R., & Stoiber, K. C. (2002). Evidence-based interventions in school psychology: Conceptual foundations of the procedural and coding manual of Division 16 and the Society for the Study of School Psychology Task Force. *School Psychology Quarterly, 17,* 341–389.

Kubicek, F. C. (1994). Special education reform in light of select state and federal court decisions. *Journal of Special Education, 28,* 27–43.

Lopez, E. (1997). The cognitive assessment of limited English proficient and bilingual children. In D. P. Flanagan, J. L. Genshaft, & P. L. Harrison (Eds.), *Contemporary intellectual assessment: Theories, tests, and issues* (pp. 503–516). New York: Guilford Press.

Lopez, R. (1997). The practical impact of current research and issues in intelligence test interpretation and use for multicultural populations. *School Psychology Review, 26,* 249–254.

Lyon, G. R., Fletcher, J. M., Shaywtiz, S. E., Shaywitz, B. A., Wood, F. B., Schulte, A., et al. (2001). *Learning disabilities: An evidence-based conceptualization.* Washington, DC: Fordham Foundation.

Lyon, G. R., Shaywitz, S. E., & Chhabra, V. (2004). Evidence-based reading policy in the United States: How scientific research informs instructional practice. In D. Ravitch (Ed.), *Brookings papers on education policy: 2005* (pp. 198–216). Washington, DC: Brookings.

Marston, D., Muyskens, P., Lau, M., & Canter, A. (2003). Problem-solving model for decision-making with high incidence disabilities: The Minneapolis experience. *Learning Disabilities: Research and Practice, 18,* 187–200.

McBride, G., Dumont, R., & Willis, J. O. (2004). Response to intervention legislation: Have we found a better way or will we be just as confused as we have been for the last ten years? *The School Psychologist, 58,* 86–91.

McCardle, P., & Chhabra, V. (Eds.). (2004). *The voice of evidence in reading research.* Baltimore: Brookes.

McLeskey, J., & Skiba, R. (1990). Reform and special education: A mainstream perspective. *Journal of Special Education, 24,* 319–326.

Murphy, D. M. (1996). Implications of inclusion for general and special education. *Elementary School Journal, 96,* 469–494.

National Association of School Psychologists. (2000). *Professional conduct manual: Principles for professional ethics and guidelines for the provision of school psychological services.* Bethesda, MD: Author. Retrieved from www.nasponline.org/pdf/ProfessionalCond.pdf.

National Association of School Psychologists. (2002). *Rights without labels.* Position paper on the provision of services to students with disabilities. Bethesda, MD: Author.

National Association of School Psychologists. (2003). *NASP recommendations: LD eligibility and identification for IDEA reauthorization.* Bethesda, MD: Author.

National Center for Education Statistics. (2004). *The condition of education 2004.* Washington, DC: U.S. Department of Education.

National Joint Committee on Learning Disabilities. (2002). Achieving better outcomes—maintaining rights: An approach to identifying and serving students with specific learning disabilities. *NASP Communiqué, 31.*

National Reading Panel. (2000). *Teaching children to read: An evidence-based assessment of the scientific research literature on reading and its implications for reading instruction.* Washington, DC: National Institute for Literacy.

No Child Left Behind Act. (2001). Public Law 107-15.

O'Connor, R. (2003). Tiers of intervention in kindergarten through third grade. Paper presented at the Response-to-Intervention Symposium, December 4–5, 2003, Kansas City, MO. Retrieved March 9, 2004, from www.nrcld.org/html/symposium2003.

O'Malley, K. J., Francis, D. J., Foorman, B. R., Fletcher, J. M., & Swank, P. R. (2002). Growth in precursor and reading-related skills: Do low-achieving and IQ-discrepant readers develop differently? *Learning Disabilities Research and Practice, 17,* 19–35.

Ortiz, S., & Flanagan, D. P. (2002). Best practices in working with culturally diverse children and families. In A. Thomas & J. Grimes (Eds.), *Best practices in school psychology IV* (pp. 337–352). Bethesda, MD: National Association of School Psychologists.

Peltier, G. L. (1993). The regular education initiative teacher: The research results and recommended practice. *Education, 114,* 54–61.

Peterson, K. M. H., & Shinn, M. R. (2002). Severe discrepancy models: Which best explains school identification practices for learning disabilities. *School Psychology Review, 31,* 459–476.

Polaha, J. A., & Allen, K. D. (1999). A tutorial for understanding and evaluating single-subject methodology. *Proven Practice, 1,* 73–77.

Pressley, M., Duke, N. K., & Boling, E. (2004). The educational science and scientifically based instruction we need: Lessons from reading research and policymaking. *Harvard Educational Review, 74,* 30–62.

Purdum, T. S. (1998, June 3). California passes measure to limit bilingual schools. *New York Times, 147* (Issue 51177), p. A1.

Reschly, D. J. (1997). Utility of individual ability measures and public policy choices for the 21st century. *School Psychology Review, 26,* 234–241.

Salvia, J., & Ysseldyke, J. E. (2004). *Assessment in special and inclusive education* (9th ed.). Boston: Houghton Mifflin.

Sanetti, L. H., & Kratochwill, T. R. (2005). Treatment integrity assessment within a problem-solving model. In R. Brown-Chidsey (Ed.), *Assessment for intervention: A problem-solving approach* (pp. 304–325). New York: Guilford Press.

Sattler, J. M. (2001). *Assessment of children: Cognitive applications.* San Diego: Jerome M. Sattler, Publisher.

Schatschneider, C., Francis, D. J., Carlson, C. D., Fletcher, J. M., & Foorman, B. R. (2004). Kindergarten prediction of reading skills: A longitudinal comparative analysis. *Journal of Educational Psychology, 96,* 265–283.

Semmel, M. I., & Abernathy, T. V. (1991). Teacher perceptions of the regular education initiative. *Exceptional Children, 58,* 9–24.

Semrud-Clikeman, M. (2003, December). *Neuropsychological aspects for evaluating learning disabilities.* Paper presented at the Response-to-Intervention Symposium, Kansas City, MO. Retrieved March 9, 2004, from www.nrcld.org/html/symposium2003

Shapiro, E. S. (2005). *Academic skills problems (3rd ed.): Direct assessment and intervention.* New York: Guilford Press.

Shaywitz, S. (2003). *Overcoming dyslexia.* New York: Knopf.

Shernoff, E. S., Kratochwill, T. R., & Stoiber, K. C. (2002). Evidence-based interventions in school psychology: An illustration of task force coding criteria using single-participant research design. *School Psychology Quarterly, 17,* 390–422.

Shinn, M. R. (1989). *Curriculum-based measurement: Assessing special children.* New York: Guilford Press.

Shinn, M. R. (1998). *Advanced applications of curriculum-based measurement.* New York: Guilford Press.

Shinn, M. R. (2005). Identifying and validating academic problems in a problem-solving model. In R. Brown-Chidsey (Ed.), *Assessment for intervention: A problem-solving approach* (pp. 219–246). New York: Guilford Press.

Shinn, M. R., Collins, V. L., & Gallagher, S. (1998). Curriculum-based measurement and its use in a problem solving model with students from minority backgrounds. In M. R. Shinn (Ed.), *Advanced applications of curriculum-based measurement* (pp. 143–174). New York: Guilford Press.

Siegel, L. (2003). IQ-discrepancy definitions and the diagnosis of LD. *Journal of Learning Disabilities, 36,* 2–4.

Siegel, L. S., & Himel, N. (1998). Socioeconomic status, age, and the classification of dyslexics and poor readers: The dangers of using IQ scores in the definition of reading disability. *Dyslexia, 4,* 90–105.

Snow, C. E., Burns, M. S., & Griffin, P. (Eds.). (1998). *Preventing reading difficulties in young children.* Washington, DC: National Academy Press.

Spear-Swerling, L., & Sternberg, R. J. (1996). *Off track: How poor readers become "learning disabled."* Boulder, CO: Westview Press.

Speece, D. L., Case, L. P., & Molloy, D. E. (2003). Responsiveness to general education instruction as the first gate to learning disabilities identification. *Learning Disabilities: Research and Practice, 18*, 147–156.

Stage, S. A., Abbott, R. D., Jenkins, J. R., & Berninger, V. W. (2003). Predicting response to early reading intervention from verbal IQ, reading-related language abilities, attention ratings, and verbal IQ–word reading discrepancy. *Journal of Learning Disabilities, 36*, 24–34.

Stanovich, K. E. (1991). Discrepancy definition of reading disability: Has intelligence led us astray? *Reading Research Quarterly, 26*, 7–29.

Stanovich, K. E. (1993). It's practical to be rational. *Journal of Learning Disabilities, 26*, 524–533.

Stanovich, K. E. (2000). *Progress in understanding reading: Scientific foundations and new frontiers.* New York: Guilford Press.

Steege, M. (1997). Encopresis and enuresis. In G. Baer, K. Minke, & A. Thomas (Eds.), *Children's Needs III: Development, Problems and Alternatives* (pp. 879–885). Washington, DC: National Association of School Psychologists.

Steege, M., Brown-Chidsey, R., & Mace, F. C. (2002). Best practices in evaluating interventions. In A. Thomas & J. Grimes (Eds.), *Best practices in school psychology IV* (pp. 517–534). Bethesda, MD: National Association of School Psychologists.

Steege, M., Davin, T., & Hathaway, M. (2001). Reliability and accuracy of a performance-based behavioral recording procedure. *School Psychology Review, 30*, 252–262.

Steege, M., & Wacker, D. (1995). Best practices in evaluating the effectiveness of applied interventions. In A. Thomas & J. Grimes (Eds.), *Best Practices in School Psychology III* (pp. 625–636). Washington DC: National Association of School Psychologists.

Stein, M., Carnine, D., & Dixon, R. (1989). Direct instruction: Integrating curriculum design and effective teaching practice. *Intervention in School and Clinic, 33*, 227–235.

Stein, M., Stuen, C., Carnine, D., & Long, R. M. (2001). Textbook evaluation and adoption. *Reading and Writing Quarterly, 17*, 5–24.

Stuebing, K. K., Fletcher, J. M., LeDoux, J. M., Lyon, G. R., Shaywitz, S. E., & Shaywitz, B. A. (2002). Validity of IQ–discrepancy classifications of reading disabilities: A meta-analysis. *American Educational Research Journal, 39*, 469–518.

Swanson, H. L., Harris, K. R., & Graham, S. (Eds.). (2003). *Handbook of learning disabilities.* New York: Guilford Press.

Swanson, H. L. & Sachse-Lee, C. (2000). A meta-analysis of single-subject-design intervention research for students with LD. *Journal of Learning Disabilities, 33*, 114–137.

Sweet, R. W. (2004). The big picture: Where we are nationally on the reading front and how we got here. In P. McCarde & V. Chhabra (Eds.), *The voice of evidence in reading research* (pp. 13–46). Baltimore: Brookes.

Syracuse Public Schools. *Intervention central.* Retrieved from www.interventioncentral.org/index.shtml

Task Force on Evidence-Based Interventions in School Psychology [Sponsored by Division 16 of the American Psychological Association and the Society for the Study of School Psychology]. (2003, June). *Procedural and Coding Manual for Review of Evidence-Based Interventions.* Retrieved from www.sp-ebi.org/_workingfiles/EBImanual1.pdf

Tatum, B. D. (1997). *Why are all the black kids sitting together in the cafeteria? and other conversations about race: A psychologist explains the development of racial identity* (rev. ed.). New York: Basic Books.

Taylor, R. L., & Richards, S. B. (1997). Teacher perceptions of inclusive settings. *Teaching Exceptional Children, 29*, 50–55.

Telzrow, C. F., McNamara, K., & Hollinger, C. L. (2000). Fidelity of problem-solving implementation and relationship to student performance. *School Psychology Review, 29,* 443–461.

Tilly, W. D., III. (2002). Best practices in school psychology as a problem-solving enterprise. In A. Thomas & J. Grimes (Eds.), *Best practices in school psychology IV* (pp. 21–36). Bethesda, MD: National Association of School Psychologists.

Tilly, W. D., III. (2003, December). *How many tiers are needed for successful prevention and early intervention? Heartland Area Education Agency's evolution from four to three tiers.* Paper presented at the Response-to-Intervention Symposium, Kansas City, MO. Retrieved March 9, 2004, from www.nrcld.org/html/symposium2003

Torgeson, J. K. (2003, December). *Operationalizing the response to intervention model to identify children with learning disabilities: Specific issues with older children.* Paper presented at the Response-to-Intervention Symposium, Kansas City, MO. Retrieved March 9, 2004, from www.nrcld.org/html/symposium2003

U.S. Department of Education, Office of Elementary and Secondary Education. (2002a). *Guidance for the reading first program.* Retrieved October 12, 2004 from www.ed.gov/programs/readingfirst/guidance.doc.

U.S. Department of Education, Office of Elementary and Secondary Education. (2002b). *No Child Left Behind: A desktop reference.* Washington, DC: Author.

U.S. Department of Education, Institute of Education Sciences. (2004). *What Works Clearinghouse.* Retrieved April 27, 2004, from www.w-w-c.org/

Vaughn, S., & Fuchs, L. S. (2003). Redefining learning disabilities as inadequate response to instruction: The promises and potential problems. *Learning Disabilities: Research and Practice, 18,* 137–146.

Vellutino, F. R., Scanlon, D. M., & Lyon, G. R. (2000). Differentiating between difficult-to-remediate and readily remediated poor readers: More evidence against the IQ–achievement discrepancy definition for reading disability. *Journal of Learning Disabilities, 33,* 223–238.

Villa, R. A., & Thousand, J. S. (1996). Teacher and administrator perceptions of heterogeneous education. *Exceptional Children, 63,* 29–46.

Watson, T. S., & Steege, M. W. (2003). *Conducting school-based functional behavioral assessments: A practitioner's guide.* New York: Guilford Press.

Weisz, J. R., & Hawley, K. M. (1999). Finding, evaluating, refining, and applying empirically supported treatments for children and adolescents. *Journal of Clinical Child Psychology, 27,* 206–217.

Williams, P. B., & Carnine, D. W. (1981). Relationship between range of examples and of instructions and attention in concept attainment. *Journal of Educational Research, 74,* 144–148.

Willig, A. (1985). A meta-analysis of selected studies on the effectiveness of bilingual education. *Review of Educational Research, 55,* 269–317.

Wright, W. E. (2004). What English-only really means: A study of the implementation of California language policy with Cambodian-American students. *International Journal of Bilingual Education and Bilingualism, 7,* 1–23.

Index